CITY ADVENTURES

Dave Ruse

This book is dedicated to the nicest and most helpful man I know: my father, Leslie Charles Ruse . . . fame at last, Dad.

ACKNOWLEDGEMENTS

A special thanks must go to the following: Val and Arthur Bull for all their typing, friendly support and endless cups of tea; Alison Moore for all the typing, spelling and grammar lessons; Sir Winston Churchill Trust for their help in giving me the opportunity to travel to research for this book; Christa Koller for her photographs on pages 39,43, 97 and 70. The following people have contributed in many ways and have given me some of the ideas for the basis of this book.

Garry Mansfield
Roger Homyer
Danny Greer
Steven Greer
John Weinstock
Julia Holmyard
Steve Rose
Brendan Geary
Martin Cusselle
Pete Fidgett
Phil Burton
Danny Clark
Greg Ship
Paul Patterson
Andrew Noakes
Danny Dawson
Graham North
S.D. Beresford
Paul Wallett
Dorothy Day
Peter Newton
Stephen Elliot
Barry O'Brien
Marcus Bailie
Terry Kinsella
Dominique Wright
Nick Chetwood
Jill Rose
Mike Stock
Liza Bruml
Carol Scott
S. Winterton
Vic Brown
Ron Moore
Eogan Carter
Mandy Freeman
Mark Freeman
Andrew Mitchell
John Quinliven
Keith Hartle
Peter Emms
Pat Mee
Elissa Levine
George Lopez
Eve Wright
Paul Liniham
Greg Hicky
Mathew Morgan
Kim & Steve
Graham Hart
Mike Coyne
Chloë Sayers
Marianne Lagrange
Leslie P. Ruse
Geoff Oldfield
Heather Harbinson
David Byrne
Robert Byrne
Damion Magee
Barney Magee
Joyce Lynch
Greg Owen
Ron White
Save the Children Fund
Belfast Community Circus
RAMOAM
Corrymeela Centre

The many young people I met in Jamaica, New York, Mexico, and Ireland.

First published 1989

Paul Chapman Publishing Ltd
144 Liverpool Road
London N1 1LA

British Library Cataloguing in Publication Data
Ruse, Dave
City adventures.
1. Group activities
I. Title
790.1'5
ISBN 1-85396-048-9

Typeset by Burns & Smith, Derby
Printed and bound in Great Britain by Butler & Tanner Ltd, Frome and London

CONTENTS

FOREWORD

The importance and value of adventure and play in the development and growth of young people has long been recognised in this country which has pioneered the Outward Bound movement, the Duke of Edinburgh's Award Scheme and children's play and recreation. Only recently have we begun however to recognise and actively provide, not only for a diversity of needs throughout the community, but also in relation to ways in which the neighbourhood environment can be used for activity.

In work with young people today there is a widespread and growing movement which is seeking to make more of opportunities which exist, are feasible and valid – even in the most unlikely of inner city settings. Learning to explore and value one's neighbourhood, through fun and the creation of excitement, adventure and challenge is an important process. It should not be seen as an inferior alternative, a method of simply occupying young people or as a way of keeping them out of trouble.

Set in the wider contexts of education, recreation and the therapies, institutions and organisations can identify the very positive benefits of such activities in a variety of learning situations in work with young people and rehabilitation programmes with older age groups. In the case of the former and at a basic or fundamental level, it may be necessary to actively foster stimulating and exciting play activity as a counter to the negative sides of television, the video and computer games, increasingly aimed at young people in the technological age. Showing young people how to play, how to have fun in the outdoors, how to react to each other may surprisingly enough, need to be actively encouraged. The blunting of senses, passiveness and the stultifying effects of over indulgence will result if left to chance. The local outdoor setting, the adventure and challenge approach has been used again as a vital stage in the process of helping hardened ex-offenders reintegrate with and develop inter-personal skills necessary to survive in society. It is strongly suspected that in such cases childhood and opportunities for play have been forshortened and expressions of emotion surpressed.

This compendium of adventure games, the second by this author is likely to have many and varied uses. It will doubtless also have its critics. There will be those who cannot accept the range of practices advocated or see the need to provide this level of adventure and challenge activity set against the formal activity provision which exists. Others will be fearful on grounds of safety and well being. 'Aims and uses of this book', together with the section on 'safety' should be read and re-read. The author is at pains to stress the need for supervision and safe practice. Another facet of safety worth considering is that referred to by Lawrence Hills – who states that:

> A naked infant in the dust of a Third World country, pretending that a row of date stones is a camel caravan is mentally safer than one staring hour after hour at a colour TV screen.

Thank you, Dave Ruse, for this contribution to the 'tool box of the practitioners', and let us hope that the 'gatekeepers' in our society will allow the ideas to flourish.

Roger Orgill
May 1989

AIMS AND USES OF THIS BOOK

I hope this book will be useful to a very large and varied range of people: parents running play schemes, teachers, youth workers, play workers, uniformed groups; those involved with probation and intermediate treatment work; organisers of outdoor pursuit centres; highly trained specialist instructors with high-tech equipment; and, of course, the young people themselves.

I have not separated activities and games for able-bodied people and people with a disability of some kind. The games in this book are for everyone. Of course, some people will be able to cope with certain games and not with others. A game suitable for a deaf person may be useless to a blind person. What one person in a wheelchair cannot do another person in a wheelchair might manage. This also applies to able-bodied people. I have written the book with all sorts of people in mind – young and old, fat and thin, male and female, rich and poor, academic and 'physical', fast learner and slow learner – as all of these have contributed with their ideas.

The activities are aimed mainly at the 10–20 year age-group, but a lot of games can be adapted and used with younger children, and a lot of older adults can have some fun too. The way this book is used will depend on the individual. You may be short of ideas and can use the book as a reference to dip into if the weather is bad; there may be a piece of waste land nearby that you want to use. You may have lots of your own ideas, but could benefit from seeing other new ones and using other types of terrain. There is always something new around the corner! Personally I shall use this book – even though I have compiled it – because I forget things, and because I sometimes have a 'blank' day when I'm working with a group.

I've tried not to go into every detail in explaining each game and activity, because it's very important for the people playing them to adapt them to their own area and local conditions. They are intended as stimulating ideas for you to use as starting points. Your own personal touch in getting the group involved and interested is the real skill. Some activities will work, some will fall flat. Proficiency in using games and activities with groups develops with practice, so I advise you to try a few simple games at first and build up gradually to more adventurous missions and adventures. The result to aim for is that the game was completely safe; that the players have enjoyed themselves, and may have learnt something; that nothing has been seriously damaged; and that no one has been left out of the group.

The games and activities in this book are for use in large towns and cities, which all vary in what they have to offer. Some cities are by the sea; some have large parklands with outcrops of rock (like Central Park in New York); some will have only a maze of streets, rubbish tips and waste land. But if you have a club in a lovely part of the countryside, you too can use the book. (I have even seen copies of my last book, *Canoe Games* (A & C Black), in Holloway women's prison, and now the Royal Marines are using it.)

There are many reasons why this book has been written. I will mention a few. Most young people living in the city will spend about 95 per cent of their lives in it, so it is important that they come to terms with their environment and use it, rather than let it use them. In this book I try to open people's eyes to what is around them, to take a fresh look at their environment, which with imaginaton and creativity can 'become' almost anything. Just because an object was made for one purpose doesn't mean it can't be used for many others. Most of the activities in this book can be done on a low budget, and some with no money at all. This is a *physical* book that uses people's minds and bodies - unlike the current craze for computers, where people sit in front of a TV screen for days on end and wouldn't leave the house unless it caught fire. Computers do have an important role in education, but the physical side seems to have become devalued. I believe that the body needs to 'think' and move. Lots of games and activities in this book make players use their minds and bodies to work out problems. Because they are enjoying themselves, this activity will stimulate their imagination to create new strategies for dealing with situations.

I want this book to be educational by encouraging people to have fun and play as they learn and develop living skills. In a confused world in which some are less fortunate than others, the 'win-or-else' mentality in sports can give the wrong impression of what they are really about, and can turn a person off for life; but with a well-thought-out plan of fun and instruction, that same person could be hooked for ever. Some people have a real fear of certain activities, especially if they involve water or if they seem ultra physical. Some of the games in this book – played safely but in a light-hearted way – can break down those fears, whereas a more structured approach might only increase them. Even the most 'boring' subjects in school can be made exciting and memorable. A history lesson about the River Thames can really come to life if you visit a museum on the subject and then afterwards take a boat ride down the river, pointing out the scenes of its gory past. Better still, go by canoe – to feel it, smell it, see it and touch it – a powerful and exciting way to learn.

Bringing street trends into the classroom in conjunction with a school subject can grab the students' attention. With careful observation and skill, some potentially destructive activities can be adapted into creative ones thereby gaining a positive image in the local community for the young people concerned. Many activities can be practised in a fun, learning way before they are actually needed in real life: rescue techniques; ways of looking after each other; coping with the elements; camping, or just surviving. Some skills can be practised before trips away, such as putting a tent up in the park and having a picnic, practising a canoe portage that might have to be done on a river if a tree has fallen in, or crawling in and out of obstacles and old dumped cars. Many of these skills can be practised simply for the sheer enjoyment of them.

Many of the ideas in this book could be adapted for sponsored events, rather than the usual long walk through streets and squares. A sponsored event needn't last all day – it could be arranged so that people give money per minute for a silly event such as doughnut eating, or how many cups of tea you can drink in an hour.

I hope the fun and games in this book will be of educational value and that the skills learnt will help in many sports, emergency situations, school teaching, domestic independence, and with other day-to-day problems. I hope, too, that it will lead many people to take a new pride in their environment and look at it with concern. Any way in which people can learn to live richer and fuller lives in the city must be positive. You have to learn how to survive and have fun in the city, otherwise it can run your life without you knowing it.

SOURCES FOR THE BOOK

Since the age of fifteen I have worked in about thirty different youth organisations, picking up ideas and activities to use with young people. These organisations have included centres catering both for people with a particular disability, and for the able-bodied. I have worked in schools, play centres, youth clubs, summer camps, uniformed groups, church clubs, water sports, pursuit centres, prisons and remand homes running alternative systems. Some clubs have been a real pleasure to be a part of, and some have been so 'heavy' I've had to walk home with a rolling-pin for protection, as a bad night could lead to a worker being attacked by a group or an individual who could well be high on something.

Over the years, working alongside so many terrific colleagues, I have managed to pick up many sensible ideas and practices. Many of the games in the book are drawn from my own experience and ideas, but I see myself also as a compiler of information from various other sources.

I have often thought that there is a general lack of ideas to use with young people. Most of the game books I have seen have dealt more with the folk lore behind an activity, or the twenty-one different variations of a game that exist around the country. This seems to me to be out of touch, ultra safe and rather too stuffy for streetwise kids. When I was half-way through my first book, *Canoe Games*, I realised there was little material available on land-based activities – so I started this book. I wrote letters to all the people who had helped with the previous book, and put articles in different sports magazines asking for ideas. The results from this were poor, but the letters I did receive were very worthwhile. I always carry a small notebook, so when I came across an activity I would write it down. The ideas could come from children playing, or from seeing some adults messing around on a building site, or surveyors measuring the roads.

If something catches my eye, I try to convert it into an activity. Any time I was abroad I would look out for new ideas to add interest to the book and to try to bring activities normally done in the countryside and mountain locations to the city – e.g. orienteering, rambles and many more. Many of my colleagues work in a similar way. Most ideas come from simply walking around the streets with an open mind and a keen eye.

In 1987 I was fortunate enough to be awarded a Winston Churchill Memorial Trust Travelling Fellowship, which allowed me to spend a great deal of time travelling to New York, Mexico and Jamaica to observe young people being creative in their play. Other places where I spent time were Belfast, Iceland, Germany, Scotland, Wales and areas of northern England, all of which provided me with new inspiration. Many of these places have particular problems, which I find can often stimulate creativity of some kind.

As I've been writing this book I realise it's very close to becoming an echo of my own childhood, which was lived on the streets, using everything around me. As a child I spent hours playing in old houses, turning them into camps and clubhouses. Friends and I would talk of what we wanted to do when we were older and the things that were going on around us. I clearly remember commenting on the different ways children and some adults see and do things. For example, take a piece of waste land: a child will use all the old bits of wood to make huts, go-karts, guns etc. Every lump, bump and brick will be something to use in adventure. Put adults in the same area and they will tidy up, burn all the wood and then close the area down and leave it empty. When I was young my father always brought home different things for me to play with, left over from what he had used to decorate shop windows. I could make anything out of those odds and ends. It is certainly true that some kids will play more with the box than with the present inside.

Apart from ideas from my childhood, the main source of inspiration for this book has been the great bunch of boys and girls I have worked with over the years, who are now good friends.

Responding to the activities in this book, some people will say 'I've done that,' or 'We used to do it as kids.' Others may even ask 'What is the point? It's stupid, destructive and a waste of time.' I have tried to show the positive, creative and educational side of this type of play. I hope that many people will enjoy the games and activities here, and use them creatively and safely. The book is intended as a stimulus, and is not meant to be the final word on the subject. Your own imagination and approach will make these games work for you.

SAFETY

Games and adventures should be exciting, fun, challenging, demanding, and sometimes just plain silly. Whatever activity you choose, it is the responsibility of the person in charge, and of the players, to minimise the risk element both before and during the event. One hundred per cent safety from any sort of accident is impossible, but as teachers, youth workers, play leaders, instructors or parents, it is up to us to pick the right sort of activity for the ability of the group, and to adapt it to the area we are going to use.

The games in this book are mainly intended to be played by groups which are supervised and organised by a responsible group leader. For some games, expert knowledge (such as life-saving or climbing skills) is essential for safety. Most, if not all the games will be more likely to be fun if they are planned with forethought.

Safety covers many areas: personal safety; the safety of other people, whether they are players or passers-by in the streets; and the safety of equipment and surroundings. Preparation, planning and forethought are essential for every activity, from a simple, quick game in the school playground, to an all-night activity on the streets of a big city. The level of preparation will vary, for example, from making sure there is no broken glass on the ground to weeks of contacting parents and helpers, arranging patrols and cars for cover, working out routes, plotting meeting points and even informing the police of your intentions.

If you are new to these types of adventure games, start small and simple to gain the confidence and skills that come with practice. Don't bite off more than you can chew! The activities are intended to stimulate ideas and give you a rough idea of what to do. It would be impossible to write down every detail, because what suits one environment won't necessarily suit another. So, *adapt* and *use common sense*. Risks are a fact of life. It is part of a young person's education to learn to recognise dangers and how to cut them down to an acceptable level.

Preparation and planning are extremely important. So, too, is a watchful eye during the event's to monitor how everything is going, and to make sure that the fun never overrides the acceptable safety level.

Here are some guidelines:

1 Select the *right level* of activity for the individuals involved.

2 Check that all ground, floors or local enviroment are *safe and suitable for use.*

3 Any equipment must be in *good working condition*, whether this is top-class climbing gear or a plank of wood for you to stand on.

4 Indoor activities can also have many danger areas, so check the play area and surrounding objects for *potential hazards.*

5 Any activity around swimming pools, streams, rivers, ponds or reservoirs needs people with *life-saving skills* in attendance. (For advice contact the Royal Life-Saving Society.)

6 On wasteland, *always check* for glass, holes in the ground and nails in wood. Never open or go near rubbish in bags as these could contain decaying matter, sharp objects or used needles.

7 When on the street, never let the activity get out of control, so that road safety is forgotten. Constantly remind the group, and introduce penalty points as part of the activity, to make them take note.

8 Any adventure trips should have the permission of the parents or guardian if participants are under eighteen years of age.

9 Night activities need good planning. This involves parental permission, keeping in small groups all the time, carrying contact phone numbers in case of trouble, and a letter of explanation, just in case the police ask! Liaise with the local police, check routes beforehand and arrange regular meeting places to keep in touch.

10 You must always know exactly how many people are involved in an activity. Check before and after the event to make sure that no one is missing.

11 Have a first-aider at hand.

12 Consider your own safety, the safety of other players, and that of third parties walking past.

13 Property and equipment should be looked after, cleaned and returned in good condition after use. Any damage or breakage should be reported.

14 Depending on the activity, the person in charge will have to decide whether to participate or separate themselves from it. Whichever you decide, you must always keep an eye on the game's progress and keep it under control.

15 Play must never override safety.

Common sense goes a long way!

The games and activities in this book have been tested in practice by an experienced person. However, neither the author nor the publisher can accept any legal responsibility or liability for any accidents that may occur as a result of careless supervision of games.

FOUND OBJECTS

The city is absolutely packed with objects everywhere. They may be inside or outside – you are surrounded by them. There are objects of all shapes and sizes: natural objects such as branches, leaves and rocks; and man-made articles such as plastic buckets or broom handles. Some objects are large, some are small. You may need only one, or perhaps thousands for your particular project. They may be rubbish that has been thrown out, left behind by builders or dumped out at the back of a large factory. But although we may call it rubbish, very few things are completely useless and cannot be re-used, repaired, recycled or put to another and totally different use. Just walk around the streets of any modern city and you will see large metal skips absolutely bulging with tables, chairs, lampshades and prams, amongst many other things. (I once got a ten-speed bike from a skip – it just needed new forks.) The people who go around collecting on the dustcarts have certainly got their heads screwed on the right way, and have a sharp eye for good-quality gear. This could include metal for scrap, objects to sell, and, of course, the teddy bear that ends up tied to the radiator of the truck.

There is an endless variety of uses for these objects. In this chapter I have selected a range of ideas, but these are not the whole story. Objects can be used in the art room, sculpture class, or for making vehicles such as go-karts and scooters. They can be used in games like treasure hunts, or as objects to be knocked down, such as tin cans on a home-made firing range. If you look over a few waste areas you will probably find a young persons' hideaway or secret camp, made from stuff they found lying around them – perhaps from corrugated sheets and wood, the interior furnished with old car seats, a cardboard box as a TV and so on.

Some objects have more potential use than others, such as milk crates or the plastic bread trays that you can see everywhere doing a different job to the one they were intended for. (I had better not mention shopping trollies!) I'm expecting to see lots of new activities with the latest waste products – such as the bubble wrap that protects delicate objects.

Once when I was working in a very sport-orientated American summer camp for children, I noticed a small group of about eight lads whom everyone else called 'The Wets'. They hated sport and competitive stuff, preferring the arts and crafts. One day I got them all together and we decided to make a Viking ship in the forest, where the empty oil drums, old dustbin lids, chairs and waste wood were dumped. Over a couple of weeks we had done a really good job: the ship looked great, although a bit out of place in the forest. Then the boss found out about the project and gave me an earful: the children's parents had paid thousands of dollars to send them to an organised camp, *not* to see them stuck on a rubbish dump! When I explained at some length that the rubbish was not decaying, just objects lying around; that the kids had been unhappy each year up to now at the camp; and that we should cater for all needs, so that everyone would want to come again – he softened up a little, and even got us a tractor to drag the ship out on to the lake. We paddled it, sailed it, swam from it and had lots of picnics on it in the middle of the lake.

You can also use objects that are not rubbish, such as tables, chairs, brooms and buckets, and return them afterwards. (Mind you, it's a good idea to get permission first!) If your club needs a few things – wood for the craft lessons, or more furniture – then, if funds are low, you can have an adventure in a game of skip hunting (skipology), looking around the streets for what you need. For example, a piece of good hardwood might be just the thing for the bit of the door that was broken at the last disco.

Almost anything can be used. When I see a child playing in the soil with a matchbox and making noises like a bulldozer, I know he has a healthy imagination. But you do have to be careful with things like drums or liquid containers in case they still have traces of dangerous chemicals in them; or any objects that have sharp edges. Watch out for broken glass and other dangerous objects. Members of the group must learn to look and think first, before touching. Hygiene and safety are vital; keep away from old, decaying rubbish and bags full of trash. Solid objects are best for re-use. You can save bottle tops, bubble wrap and drink cans from around your home. Your area may have a scrap project or recycling centre where factories are throwing away lots of odd bits, such as dolls' arms, buttons, tyres and lots more objects with potential alternative uses.

Even the ordinary bonfire can be a focus for group activity – you need not wait until 5 November. You could burn off the rubbish in the club's backyard, or sit around it at the end of the day to chat about this and that. Always make sure the fire can't set anything else alight; keep an eye on the wind, and make sure the fire is put out completely before you leave.

THE GAMES

HEAD CARRYING

No, you don't carry heads, but you do carry gear *on* your head. In different countries, all around the world, people have developed the skill of carrying loads on their heads – from a simple pot to a pile of crates. They do not need to use their hands to keep these loads on their heads; instead, they just use balance. With larger loads they often wear some sort of hat.

You could try this game with some small loads to begin with that will not break if, or should I say when, you drop them. Then build up to larger loads. When you get good at it you can go on walkabout up and down staircases, through double doors and any other obstacles you see en route. If you want a hat and don't have one you can use a towel coiled on your head.

CARDBOARD HUTS

This activity can be done at any time of the year. If you have a local factory that has waste cardboard in the yard, ask if you can use it. You can use just a few boxes to make a simple hut or lots of boxes to build a whole new clubhouse, using string or tape to put it together. You could have a theme like outer space or medieval knights; large groups could then make a space station or a castle.

If the weather is a little cold you could make the hut as warm as possible and have a cup of tea in it, or make a simple meal. (Be careful not to burn the hut down!) In warmer weather you could stay on your club site all night in the hut, or take the cardboard to another site, rig it up and then stay there for the night. Make sure the position of the hut is not going to put you in danger through somebody mistaking your hut for rubbish, for example a dustman on his early morning clean-up.

CARDBOARD EGGS

In this game you can play indoors or out. The idea is to have a strong cardboard box, a blindfold and, of course, some players! One brave player wears the blindfold and gets into the cardboard box. The others lightly tape the box up, then pick it up and walk away with it, going all over the place trying to upset the co-ordination of the person in the box. When the box is put down the player has to break out of this egg-like structure (still wearing the blindfold) and find his/her way back to the starting place. The others don't say a word unless there is any danger. They stay with the blindfolded player as they try to get back by remembering, listening, feeling and even smelling. When the player finds the start, the next person can have a go.

Do not tape them up so tightly that they can't get out, and make sure there are some holes in the box to let the air in. Also, be careful where you leave the box - at the top of a staircase would be dangerous!

CARDBOARD TUNNEL

Go out and find as many cardboard boxes as possible and bring them back. Open the ends up on all of them, then join them up together into one long tube or tunnel by slipping one into the other so there is an overlap of a few inches. Then you all line up at one end and crawl through it, get out of the tube at the other end, run back to the start and do it again.

You could have two teams, one each at opposite ends. On the word 'GO' you all have to rush through the tunnel, passing the other team in the middle. You could extend the game by having two or three tunnels, one after another. Maybe you could make lots of tunnels and invent a new game.

CARDBOARD SLEIGH

Find one really large cardboard box, open the lid and the bottom, then cut one of the seams so you end up with one large sheet of cardboard. This game needs a minimum of two players and a maximum of about four. The idea is for one or two players to sit on the cardboard mat while the others hold an edge and run them along the ground on the mat. After a while the runners will get very tired; this is a good sign to change places. MIND THEM PUDDLES!!

CARDBOARD BOX ROLLING

A group of you need to go out and find a large cardboard box each. When you all have one, open the ends up, then get inside and lie down. The game is simple: all you do is roll around and have fun. You can double or treble up in one box and roll around together. When all the boxes are ripped to pieces except one, take it to a grass slope, all get in it and have one final roll. Don't forget to clean up the mess afterwards, and keep away from traffic!

TYRE BOWLS

In the past, bowls may have seemed to be a more mature sport for older people. Not now! This game may not get new blood into the traditional sport, but it should give some an enjoyable time. You need lots of tyres all the same size, except one which is smaller. You play the game like bowls but with very simple rules. One player rolls the small tyre away until it stops and falls down – this is the marker or jack. Each player has two or three larger tyres, and from the point the small tyre was thrown they each have a go to see how close they can roll their tyres to the marker. The player with the closest tyre wins. If a player lays his/her tyre on top of another player's which is the closest to the jack, the one on top wins. To start the next game, you simply throw the marker again to a new area. The person who won the previous game throws, and one of the other players starts first. You can play on a flat area or one with obstacles and bumps to give interest. This game could be played in an evening league.

GIANT TYRE ROLLING

The idea in this game is to find the biggest tyre you can and play rolling it. You stand it upright and give it a big push to see how far it will roll and how straight it will run. Another activity with it is to keep pushing it to see how long you can keep it on the move, as it goes where you want for a while and then turns off and tries to do its own thing. If you are young or small you can use a smaller, lighter tyre or bike wheel. We used to roll our tyre to the nearest hill and let it loose from the top.

You have to be careful to make sure there are no people or parked cars in the way, as a tyre can do a lot of damage if it hits someone or something; and never play near a road, as the tyre might roll into the road and cause an accident. When you have finished, hide your tyre to play with it another day; then look at the colour of your hands and clothes!

TYRE-ROLLING COURSE

In this game you need lots of tyres of any size and a course like a BMX track, or one you have made yourselves with a ramp,etc. You simply roll a tyre and see who can push the tyre around the course the fastest.

DISTANCE TYRE PUSH

This tyre game is played on a large flat area of ground. All you need are a few tyres. First, have a starting line; then, either one at a time or all together, push the tyres to see how far they will go – the straighter the better, but it's hard to get a tyre to keep going straight when it slows down.

TYRE-ROLLING NOUGHTS AND CROSSES

Why use tyres to play noughts and crosses when you can do it on paper with a ballpoint pen? Read on! First draw a large box with chalk on the flat ground, 9 feet by 9 feet. Mark out inside this box nine boxes at 3 feet square so that you have a giant noughts and crosses playing area. You then mark a much larger square around this one at about 29 feet square so that there is a gap of 10 feet all around the inner box. The idea is to have some white tyres and some black ones. These are the noughts and crosses, and each player has to roll them into a square from outside the larger square. The tyre must fall into a box without lying across a white line. If it does, you have to remove it and the next person tries. You play like noughts and crosses and try to get a line of three or stop the other player getting a line.

TYRE BOUNCING

There is not much to say about this other than that you need a large tyre. Sit on it and bounce as high and as far as you can. You can race each other, see who can bounce the highest, or who can keep their feet off the ground the longest. What about trying one of those giant tyres?

STONE CAN

This game can be played anywhere with found objects. All you need are a few stones and an old tin can, open at one end. The can needs to be placed on the ground, on a ledge or up high at a distance from the players. The players should be sitting in a large circle with the can in the middle, or lined up with the can 10 or 20 feet away. The idea is to grab a handful of stones, throw them one at a time, and try to get them to land in the can. If a stone goes in and then bounces out of the can, it is not counted. The aim is to count the amount of stones you get in the can as they fall in, and the one with the most is the winner.

CAN PUSH-OFF

Can push-off is a very skilful game.You play in pairs against each other and each pair needs four cans, two each. The cans need to be strong ones that you can stand on. Each player stands facing another with a two-foot gap between them. Each foot has a can under it and your legs are apart. The idea is to try to knock the other player off balance and make them fall. Both players have their hands up at chest height. To get your opponent off balance you can either slap both your hands on theirs, or pretend to and avoid them – when you do that they try to counteract against thin air. You get one point every time you get the other person off; the first one to ten wins.

There are a lot of tactics and cunning, as you will discover. But if you find it too easy you can try a variation called bumming, which is the same except that you face in opposite directions and use your bums to push – but not too hard, or you will go flying!

CAN DRUM KIT

This is for the person who is learning to play the drums but hasn't got their own set yet. The idea is to collect as many different-sized tin cans as you can, from 6 inches to 4 feet high in a variety of widths. Arrange them around you and start hitting the beat. You can use either drumsticks or your hands like bongo drums.

CAN CRAWLING

This game can be played using either two cans or four cans per player. If you use two cans you need to stand on the kerb or a low chair with a can in each hand. Your feet stay on the ledge and you hold the cans on the floor and try to walk with your hands on the cans as far out from your feet as possible, and then get back. Using four cans, put a can under each hand and foot and lie in a face-down position on top of them. You then have to travel across the floor without touching it. You cannot tie the cans to yourself. You need to juggle your weight around

while on the cans and move them along one at a time, trying not to knock them over. This could make a silly race if a lot of players line up with a target to get to.

STAN-CAN

Yes, it does sound a bit like the 'can can', but you don't have to dress up in frilly skirts and kick your legs past your ears! (Although you can if you want to.) You need an empty drink can and a watch to time a person standing on it with one leg. If the can is of super-thin metal it will add interest, as you have to stand on it a lot more carefully and not jump around so much, trying to keep your balance. The idea is to time each person from the minute they get up on the can until they fall off or put a foot down. The person who stays up the longest wins. You can make things more difficult by having to hold a cup of water and stopping the watch if any of the water spills.

TIN-CAN HIT GOLF

This is a simple idea but could be a lot of fun, and if played often enough it could improve the accuracy of your shooting. Besides your golf sticks and balls you need about ten objects, such as tin cans. All you need to do is to stand the objects up at a distance and try to knock them down by aiming and hitting the balls. The cans can be empty or full, on the ground or high up, near or far, separate or piled up. As you see, there are lots of variatons. Make sure there is nothing behind the objects to break, and no one to hit! This game can be played by one person or a small group.

JAMAICA CAN CLOGS

Each person has two drink cans. Lay a can on the ground and press your foot into its side so that it crushes around your shoe in the middle of the foot. Stamp your foot down a few times until the can is moulded to your foot and will not fall off; then do the same to the other foot so that you end up with tin cans under both feet. Now you have your clogs you can run along the street making a lot of strange noises, or even do on-the-spot tap dancing. If you get a group together you could organise a small tap-dance show.

BATH-TUBS

What *can* you do with a bath-tub? Some of the young people I know would be quite lost without theirs! Here are just a few ideas that you could build on.

1 Wash in it.
2 Turn it into a vehicle with wheels on it. The front wheels can be steered with string.
3 Land sailing tub: put some wheels on it and rig a sail to move it.
4 Bath-tub water craft: build floats around the tub until it will float with you in it. You can use paddles or oars.
5 Turn it into a giant flower-pot at the club and grow plants.
6 Giant fish bowl: make sure the plug stays in!
7 Football catcher: when the balls are kicked they have to stay in the bath and not bounce out.

It's up to you to design and construct them. To put wheels on a bathtub, you need a wooden frame to support the bath, and you put the wheels on the frame. A light plastic bath is easier to work with than steel or cast iron!

BOOT ON A ROPE

You have heard of soap on a rope; well, this is boot on a rope. All you need are a length of rope and an object like a boot. Tie the boot to the rope at one end, and get the players to make a large circle with one person in the middle. The middle person has the rope and starts to swing it in a large circle with the boot on the outside. When the boot has worked up a good momentum another player steps into the circle and has to jump over it as it comes around close to the floor. Each player has three lives, and loses one every time the boot hits them. If players are really good the boot can start to creep up from the floor so that players have to jump higher. When a player has lost all their lives he/she changes with the person in the middle.

LOG OR BARREL WALKING

Well, you've probably seen the seal at the circus or fair walking and playing on a strong ball, or the lumberjack rolling logs as they float on the big rivers in Canada. Now's your chance! You could use a round piece of a cut-down tree-trunk to start with, and then move up to one of those empty 50-gallon oil drums. You need to stand up on it and try to walk it forwards or backwards without falling off. It can be a real challenge and a lot of fun. You could put some water in the barrel so that it will roll crookedly. I wonder if anyone can juggle while walking on the barrel?

SKITTLES

You can spend hours playing skittles, but it's one of those activities that seems to get forgotten until you see someone else playing it. All you need is to collect as many tin cans as possible and mark out some lanes. Put ten cans up at one end in a triangle pattern, then find a ball or something similar to roll at the skittles. If you cannot find tin cans, anything that stands up will do.

ROAD CONES

I'm sure there are thousands of ways to use(or misuse) road cones, but here are a few simple ideas to get you thinking.

1 Marking out a playing area
2 Goalposts
3 Relay games, to run in and out of the cones as they are spaced out
4 Slalom events on skateboards, skates and push-bikes
5 Silly hats
6 Loudspeakers
7 Skittles
8 Objects to be knocked down by throwing things at them or kicking a football for shooting practice
9 How far you can throw a cone

NAME GAME

This game can be a lot of fun, and it develops your balance skills. It could be used with a group who are new to each other and may not know one another's names. You need two large empty oil drums and a plank. Place the oil drums apart on a flat area of ground with the plank resting on top of them as a bridge. (You can use more drums and planks to extend the bridge if the group is large.) Get the players to line up on the plank in any order. When you are ready and standing on the bridge you have to rearrange yourselves into a given order without falling off. One possibility could be to line up in name alphabetical order, etc.

STONE BOULES

This game is very simple, and it is played in France and Spain by people of all ages. It is like bowls, where you have to get as close as possible with your ball to a smaller ball (the target) a certain distance away. But instead of rolling these balls you have to throw them underarm so that they drop as close to the target as possible. This can be played with round stones,and doesn't need a fancy lawn with players dressed up in white – in fact, it's best played on a soft, dusty or dry, muddy surface. A small group of players have five stones each and the target stone is thrown first. You can also play this using balls made from scrunched-up paper.

BOX RACE

This game is good value for money. The group divides up into pairs and each pair has two boxes. These boxes can be cardboard, wood or old milk crates. Each pair stands in the two boxes, one foot in each box, one player just behind the other. Get all the players to line up, standing in their boxes, and on the word 'GO' they have to race to another point with the boxes on their feet. You can vary the races: for example, the same teams have to race backwards, or one person has a box on each foot but has the partner on their back. You could even add props, such as the pair having to carry a bucket of water.

OBJECT MASS STAND

The idea here is to find an object like a large rock or large empty oil drum and see how many people can stand on it at the same time without anyone's foot touching the floor. Count as people get up on to

it. Make sure it is not too high off the ground so that players do not hurt themselves if they fall.

HIT THAT OBJECT

This game can be very addictive: once you start it is hard to stop, and it draws other people in. If there is some waste land near you with lots of objects and loose stones lying around, you can make a line of objects such as tin cans, plastic and glass bottles, or even a discarded teddy bear (poor thing!) Stand well back and try to knock them over by throwing stones. The objects can be on the ground or floating on water. Depending on the situation you can smash, sink or knock the objects over. If you are in a public place use plastic bottles, and if noise is a problem also leave out the tin cans. However, most large areas of waste land will be suitable.

WELLY THROWING

Have a look around local waste lands and back streets (or even ask a fisherman for his catch!) until you find old wellington boots. Even if you only get one boot between you, the game must go on. Line up in an open area with a large space in front of you. One at a time, throw the welly as far as possible; the one who throws the furthest wins. If you only have one boot, mark the spot where it lands each time. This is obviously the city equivalent to the Olympic shot put!

MILK CARTON FLICKING RACE

This simple game can be converted to many different sports with a little adaption here and there. You need some of those small half-pint milk or orange juice containers that are made out of wax-covered cardboard. Also you need some whippy thin sticks. Each player has their own stick and carton. This can be played solo, but I think two or more make it more interesting. You line up with the cartons upright on the floor with the top open, and the aim is to flick them along a marked course. You are not allowed to touch the cartons with your hands, only with the stick. The way to propel a carton is to attach the stick to the open end and flick it in the direction you wish it to travel. The course may simply be from one chalk line to another, over an obstacle course or played like a game of golf. You could even try the high jump or the long jump.

ROLLER DOOR KNOCK-OFF

This is a combat game of balance, wit and cunning. You need an old door of strong plywood, and a strong ball to place under it. The idea is to have two players standing on the door with the ball underneath in the middle, and as they move and roll around they have to try to get the other person on the ground so they are out. The winner stays on, while the next opponent issues their challenge.

THE LOCAL ENVIRONMENT

The environment is everything around us – in the country, the city or indoors. It's all those objects surrounding you, like buildings, walls, bridges, flyovers, underpasses, park benches, fences, lamp-posts and drain-hole covers, The environment around me includes dumped cars, oil cans, milk crates piled high outside the milk depot, canal walks, clean air, fumes, nice things and nasty things.

The environment can change within a few minutes' walk, or with a change in the weather. You're one hundred per cent in it, and there is no way out. All you can do is move from one part to another. I think it is very important that you use the environment without exploiting it. Your local city environment has a history and a future, and both these aspects can be used to form the basis of some activity. You could make a history lesson out of walking around interesting areas. You could have a project which aims to conserve a particular area, such as a local pond which you keep in a condition that attracts insects, birds and other plant or wildlife. The city is full of such havens that need looking after, even if it's just to stop a car park being built on top of them.

Some activities may simply involve looking at what is around you. This may be of a serious nature, or could be a very silly idea – such as counting how many windows your building has, or measuring the street as part of a bizarre treasure hunt for useless information. Some things may need improving, like a wall at the club which a mural could brighten up. You might prefer to organise a street-wise fashion show, all dressed up as drainpipes or bus stops. I used to love drawing the environment, from back alleys, early-morning markets and late-night pub scenes, to the ghost-like spectacle of a railway station last thing at night, with a couple of engines at the end of the platform.

Apart from the activities in this chapter, how about a visit to a museum, cinema, art gallery, car racing, fairground, ice skating, bowling, swimming or the ballet? Picnics are always a popular activity, organised at short notice, and can be held anywhere: in the park, on the canal, in the playground, under a bridge, on a train, up a church tower, or on your doorstep.

A lot of the games I played as a child were environmentally based. In the estate where we lived you could use the walls, fences, pipes and hop-along posts to get around the block without touching the ground. Other activities would be to hit balls up into holes where bricks were missing, or to find a local derelict house to make a camp in. If there is a tall building in your area, why not try to get permission to go to the top of it for sight-seeing? Look around you, get a few ideas for projects, then get permission and make sure they are safe and legal. The environment is all round us, so why not use it!

THE GAMES

QUIET PLACE

We don't often use our senses as well as we could, especially our hearing, but in this game you are actually trying to find a place where you do not need to use it. Mind you, to find such a place you will need to concentrate a lot on your hearing. In small groups, go off and try to find the quietest place around. It could be an indoor or outdoor project, and done during the day or the night, as all have their own particular noises. When you find your spot, all sit there for a set time and listen without making any noise. Maybe you could meet another group and compare your places by sitting in each other's in silence. It sounds an impossible game with some of the groups I know, but I'll still give it a try!

PROP PORTRAIT PHOTOGRAPHY

The idea is to take a photo of every single person in your club or school class with one particular prop. The prop can be anything, and it is given to each person in turn who is asked to do something with it while you take a picture. An example would be a pair of dark sunglasses that you can wear normally or on your knee. When everyone has been photographed you can then develop the snaps and mount them together, having fun looking at all the variations.

BACKDROP PHOTOGRAPHY

In this photography exercise you need a wall behind the subject so that you can draw or chalk up shapes, such as a car you pretend to sit in, or a large pair of wings that you stand in front of so that it looks as if you're wearing them. Take a few photos with different people posing, and then you can change the backdrop and take a few more.

PHOTO BIT

If you ask around you will probably find two or three people in the group who have those 'instant' cameras. Divide the group into small teams of three or four, and give them one loaded camera per group. You walk around the local area and take a photo of a bit of an object, or part of a building, but not *all* of it. Each person in the team can take three photos. The aim is to take the shot in such a way that it is hard for the other groups to recognise the subject. After a given time (say an hour), the groups all meet back at the club. One at a time, players show a photo while others in different groups have to guess what it is and where it was taken. You get five points for your group if you guess what a photo is, and five if no one can guess yours.

CAMERA WAR

This game needs as many instamatic cameras as you can get your hands on – ask the members a week or so beforehand. Divide the group into two halves, each with an equal number of cameras in the team. The game is played in a large area about two miles square; it should be somewhere very busy and crowded, such as a market-place. The idea is to take photos of members of the opposing team without them knowing it. As you see one of them hiding in a doorway or behind a stand, then take a photo, noting a few details such as what time it is, where you took the snap etc. If they see you, it still counts;

but try not to tell the person who has been snapped at the time, so that it is a surprise at the end when they think they have done so well. The game ends when you meet back at the club at a given time and present who has been 'got', one team at a time. The team with the most photos wins. One player cannot snap the same person twice; but two or more people can shoot a person and get a point each.

PRETEND MOTORBIKE SCRAMBLING

This is exactly the same as real motorbike scrambling – but without motorbikes. You can play this on flat land, up or down hills, inside or outside. You could even set out a special course. I usually play this down hills for fun. Simply line up everybody who is silly enough to play it, get them to hold their arms up at chest height, all make a noise that sounds like a motorbike, and on the word 'GO', you all rush off down the hill or around the circuit imitating the jumps and spills that go with scrambling.

Keep clear of the public, and have some plasters available at the end. Remember, a good scrambler always washes their bike after a scramble! This game doesn't always have to be with motorbike noises: you could be bulldozers, or even a swarm of wasps!

LOCAL SURVEYING

How well do you know your own area? Probably not as well as you think. Do you know the height of your club door, or how many steps there are down to the steet? How many yards long and wide is your street? If your club is on a hill, what is the hill's angle? How low is the bottom of the hill? How high the top?

There are very many things you don't know but could find out. You can use either very simple equipment such as a tape measure, or complicated surveying gear if you can get hold of it and know how to use it!

LOCAL COUNTING

In this game you have a simple map of part of your local area. Your aim is to find or count as many particular objects as possible. These could be churches, telephone boxes, post boxes, or even lamp-posts. Players go off in small groups to find and count them in a given time. They then report their findings, and can transfer them to a large wall chart or map, together with other groups' findings. Each week you can add to the club map. One week it could be petrol stations, and another it might be other clubs. After a while you build up a large, informative map of your 'territory'.

MAP MAKING

Many people know their local area, but if asked to give directions or draw a map they get a little lost, or the map goes off the sheet of paper. The task here is to draw a map of your local square mile on one sheet of paper. You could have a bias, such as green areas being more important on the map than streets. You might go to a park and make a map of the paths, ponds and benches. A week later you could try out each other's maps to see if they work.

MAP RACE AND READING

First, you need two road maps of your city. Divide the group into two teams and give them a map each. You decide on a place that the whole group has to get to as fast as possible on foot, not using any other form of transport. Make sure they mark down exactly where they have to get to (e.g. a McDonalds at Puke Street, West End).

When everybody is ready, the two teams are dropped off at different starting points so that they will not meet each other en route, unless they go really wrong. The starting places have to be the same distance away from the meeting place. (A simple way to do this is to use a pair of compasses to draw a circle on the map within a few miles' radius of the meeting place.) Drop off the teams in one or two mini-buses, and have a responsible person in each group with a watch to make sure that they both start at the same time. The first team to reach the destination wins. When both teams have arrived they have some lunch and discuss their journey and troubles getting there.

The trip back could be another race from the restaurant to home, finding the fastest way back. The teams leave with an interval of, say, ten minutes between them. That time is then accounted for at the other end, so you can work out which team got home in the faster time.

HIGH VIEWS

This does not mean 'intellectual'! You may live in a built-up area where it is impossible to get a good panoramic view, and where the biggest open space is the local football ground. Find a big hill, or get to the top of a tower block, and have a look around. You could take a camera or just sit and enjoy it, spotting the streets and buildings you know. Some churches have a tower, and you can ask for permission to go up and look out.

HISTORY TRAIL

If you live in a town or city that has lots of history, then you could plot a hike route that goes past the places of interest. You can stop from time to time and point out a few facts, as history is a lot more interesting when you see it for real, rather than just read about it. You don't have to walk, either. If the river goes past some interesting places, you can canoe, row or take a pleasure-boat ride. If you don't live in an area of historic interest, then you can make up an imaginary history that is full of funny rubbish and silly ideas.

ARCHAEOLOGICAL STREET WORK

Basically, this is a walk around the town with a difference – you suddenly become archaeologists. As you walk through the streets you look for an object of interest lying around, like a tin can, bottle top, roller skate or anything else you come across. You have to pretend that you live a few hundred years in the future, and all records of this found object have been lost; so you have no clue as to what it is. Each person finds an object and gives their idea of what it is, then each other member of the group gives their own ideas. The suggestions can be as silly as you like, as long as they are not accurate. When you have finished with one object, move on and look for another.

CITY BODY-BUILDING

For different reasons some young men and women like to build up or trim down their bodies. Some may be too young for the local gym, or cannot afford it. You have to be careful if you are very young, as you are still growing, but as long as you warm up, have a good variety of exercise and do not train to excess or fanatically, it should be very heatlhy. First have a stretch and then a short run to warm up, and then try this home-made course.

Have a look around the club and local park for things that are strong enough to use, such as a beam to pull up on and a park bench to do stand-ups on. In between you can do sets of press-ups and sit-ups. You can use the pavements to jump from one slab to another, missing out the one in between. Large housing estates can also be added to the circuit, using the stairs and benches. Have a look around for objects like bags of sugar or bricks to lift, instead of dumb-bells for arm work, or put a log behind your neck for squats. You must pay as much attention to good grip, stance and technique as you would in a gym, especially having a spotter in case you slip. It can be a lot of fun doing it this way in a small group. Remember, you need an experienced person around to keep an eye on things and to advise.

CAMP FINDING

In this game the idea is to go around a set area of a local estate or piece of waste land in search of a good place to make a camp or small club hut. If there are only two or three of you, then you could all work on the same one; if there are lots of you, then divide up into pairs. The two things you want to work on in this activity are: to look at the area and buildings and use them to help you; and to look around for other objects that could help you, such as a sheet of polythene or some corrugated iron. You might choose an area where two walls meet and there is a tree only a few feet away: this would provide a wind-break and act as a good base to lean your shelter against or tie things to. You may simply find an old shed or coal bunker to turn into your camp. If it is a big group, you could take turns meeting in each other's camps, or you could all make your camps as secret as possible so that, after a set time or at a whistled signal, you have to try to find the others' camps. Just make sure that you stay in the set area, and that there are no danger spots such as railways or busy roads.

SWING GARDEN GYMNASTICS

When I first saw this in Mexico, I couldn't believe my eyes. In the middle of the park was a normal everyday swing garden, but the difference was that at certain times, teenagers used it to keep fit doing gymnastics. There was a coach in charge of about twenty young men and women who were working out with the accompaniment of a large music box. There were a few dumb-bells and bendy bars around to use, but most people used the bars to pull up and do other gymnastic exercises. The group had obviously been training together for a long time, as their bodies were in tip-top condition. So the next time you pass your local swing park, think how you could use the equipment available and adapt it to a group work-out.

SCREAMING

This activity needs its own special place, which can be either a very quiet place with nobody around, or a very noisy place. Each person in the group can try screaming at the top of their voice, or the whole group can try together. It's a great way to express yourself and let off steam. Mind you, it's not recommended in built-up areas late at night – unless you like a bucket of water over your head!

THE OLYMPIC DUMP

The following Olympic events have been adapted a bit to suit a piece of waste land and a budget of nothing. You need some soft ground, grass or sand. There must be no hazards around like broken glass, so have a tidy up first.

1. 100 metre sprint: mark out start and finish lines 100 metres apart.
2. Long jump: mark a take-off point by scratching a line in the earth with a stick, and mark where each jumper lands.
3. High jump: pile up stones or bricks to make two equal piles, and balance a stick on top which will fall off if touched.
4. Javelin: make some javelins out of old, straightish branches.
5. Shot put: scratch a circle in the earth. You throw from inside this circle. Find a rock of suitable size, and use it as a shot.
6. Triple jump: use the long-jump area.
7. Hurdles: make lots of jumps along the 100 metre sprint area by laying down pipes, or planks of wood – use whatever you can find.

I'm sure you get the idea. These events can last twenty minutes or all day, and you can play them with five to thirty people. Sorry, no medals (unless you make them from milk-bottle tops)!

FALLEN TREE CHASE

When you find a large tree fallen down on its side, and it's still fresh and strong, you can play tag. One person has to catch and touch another, so that they then become the chaser. All the players have to stay on the branches and not touch the ground.

An alternative is to leave the tree when you are caught, until the next game, which starts when all the others are off the tree. The first one to have been caught is 'on' in the next game.

FEEL A TREE

Find an area in your local park with lots of trees close together. Divide up into pairs, with one person being blindfolded while the other remains 'sighted'. The sighted player leads the blindfolded one by a roundabout route to a tree and lets them feel it for two or three minutes to become familiar with its texture. You the return to the starting point, take the blindfold off and see if the person can find the tree. After they have (or have not) found it, you change places. Up to about ten minutes is enough time to allow to try to find the tree. If they can't find it in that time, show them the tree, and perhaps the route you took to it.

OCTOPUS TREE BOUNCING

Now and then a tree falls down because of strong winds or lightning, or because of disease or vandalism. We can still use the fallen tree, just as it lies with its branches parallel to the ground, like an octopus with its tentacles outstretched.

First, you climb all around it to check that it is safe and springy. If it's been on its side for years, it could have dried out and may snap. Most branches should be close to the ground or at the most about 7 feet high. The game is to hold on for safety to a branch above the one you are standing on, and start bouncing. As you get the feel of it you can move further along the branch to where it will bounce even more.

STINGING NETTLE WALK

For this incredibly silly game you need to be wearing short trousers or a skirt, or roll up your trouser legs. The idea is to walk through a patch of stinging nettles without getting stung. It *is* possible by placing your feet carefully as you move through, clearing a path. Try it yourself, or get some 'guinea pigs' to try it out for you!

NATURE DETECTIVES

This game of detectives isn't to investigate crime and follow up clues, but more to identify things in nature, such as different trees, birds, mushrooms, fish, even clouds. First you need a guide book to the topic you have decided to concentrate on. Then go to your local park to study the things you may find there; or to a reservoir, where there may be lots of different varieties of birds; or even just pop outside the club on a day that has mixed weather to see what clouds are passing overhead. You could make records of what you have found and then go out to find other things you haven't seen. So in fact, this may mean digging up a few clues as to where to find them.

GRAVEYARDS

Graveyards don't sound the most exciting places for games (you could even say they were *dead* boring). But a visit to a cemetery just to walk around and read some of the stones can be very interesting. Some really old sites, like my local one, Highgate Cemetery, give free guided tours, and they can be really spooky and full of history.

You can visit some cemeteries at night, if there are no fences or gates. You should ask for permission and explain what you are doing, show it will not be disrespectful and that no damage will occur as you will stick to the paths. The game could be to sleep in the yard for a whole night, or you could have a 'ghost hunt' with candles.

FOLLOW THE LEADER

Pick a leader that the group will follow for a given period – say ten minutes. All the players have to line up behind the leader, who has to lead the group around whilst they try to copy everything he/she does; if they don't get it right, they are out. After the set time, the next player in line takes over the leadership.

The leader can make the route easy or hard: hop along, climb over a fence, crawl through a pipe, jump in a puddle, or lie face down in the mud! (See pp. 69 for variations of this game.)

CIRCLE LINE PARTY

In London there is an underground line called the Circle Line. It goes in one big circle, so you can stay on it all the way round and get off at the same station that you got on at. I have some friends who had a party on it as the train travelled around, with other passengers getting on and off. (Don't try it during the rush hour!)

TUBE TRAIN RACE

If your city has a underground railway system like London's tube, you can have a race to a given destination. You must buy the correct ticket for the journey. You need a map of the system, and two or three teams. First, decide on a station you have to get to, and then plan different routes to get there. The idea is to see who gets there first. You are allowed to use other forms of transport. Rather than making a special journey, you could have a race to your normal destination.

SUBWAY SURFING

Hawaii is fine if you like large, smooth waves, but when it comes to a rough, bumpy ride, you will be hard pushed to find one as furious as the New York subway or the Waterloo and City Line (nicknamed 'The Drain') in London. You need to stand in the middle of a carriage in the standing area with your feet close together as if you were on a surfboard. The idea is to maintain a surfing position from when the train starts to when it stops at the next station, without having to hold on to any support. Different parts of the line give different grades of toughness, so you can have competitions at different locations. The rush hour is not a good time to do this, as the train is too heavy to get speed up and there is less room – and, of course, you get more funny looks!

AROUND THE WORLD IN HALF AN HOUR

Perhaps not around the world – more like around the estate or playground. This can be real adventure if you live in one of those really old estates with lots of buildings, coal bunkers, sheds, rubbish bins, walls and fences. All you do is start at one point and try to climb right round

the outside edge of the area without touching the ground. You don't need to climb high, as long as you are off the floor.

As you work your way round you will come across all sorts of problems that you will have to work out how to overcome. Be careful that the climb will not be too hard for the group, and that if they fall it will only be a couple of feet. If the group is young, you might only be able to do sections of the climb. If there are some very hard sections, you might need special climbing equipment and an instructor. You could take some survival gear like a plank to cross gaps, or rope to set up a swing or rope crawl. You could even carry a small pram or some tin cans with strings on and walk the difficult sections just off the ground.

The game could be played inside a big hall, climbing over the radiators, chairs and cupboards. You could try two teams climbing at the same time but in different directions, so they have to cross each other about half-way. Anyone who touches the floor loses a life, and you have three lives.

Don't forget that old pipes can come away from walls, and bricks may crumble, so you have to be careful. Don't climb high - a building can be more dangerous than a mountain. And make sure you don't trespass on private property.

WALL ROPE

If your club has a wall with no dangerous bits sticking out, and a place to secure a rope, then why not put one up? The rope hangs down the wall, touching it. The idea is to swing or run across the wall on the rope, and throw yourself from side to side. The rope has a knot at the bottom to sit on. When you get good at it, you can bounce in one go from one side to the other. You should never be more than 5 feet from the ground. Make sure you use a thick rope and the right knots to secure it.

CITY TIGHTROPE WALKING

This might send a shiver up your spine if you think of people trying to balance on a rope at a dangerous height. But you can do it safely from 2 inches above the ground, and work up to the dizzy height of 3 feet.

Here are some ways to try.

1 Scaffold walk. If you find a long scaffolding pipe lying around (or ask to borrow one from building site), you can lay it on the floor and try to walk from one end to the other without you falling off or it rolling away. If you find a long branch you can carry it as a balance bar. When you master it, you can put the ends of the pipe on milk crates to make it higher.

2 Brick walking. If you have lots of bricks lying around, line them up end to end and use them to walk along. Then turn them on their ends and try it.

3 Wall walking. If you have some low walls about 3 feet high around your club, park or street you could try walking along these and see how far you can get without falling off.

4 Rope walking. Stretch a thick rope or wire as tightly as possible between two lamp-posts or trees, at only 2 feet above the ground. The distance mustn't be too wide, as the rope will sag in the middle because you can't get it taut enough. Hold a balance bar, and off you go.

5 Scaffold plank walking. This is a good game, as it can be made progressively harder. First you lay a plank on some bricks so it is easy to walk across, and have a warm-up. Then you make it higher.

Now to make it difficult. You need two planks; stand them on their edges. You need to wedge them so they don't fall over. This will give you a width of about four inches. When you can do this easily, remove one of the planks so that players have only a 2-inch edge to walk across.

These games are not dangerous if they are kept close to the ground. You can vary what you do on the rails – use a balance bar, walk backwards, turn round and round in the middle, or hop across. Make sure your shoes are securely fastened.

CITY BACKPACK

This is going to sound stupid, but here goes. There are lots of ways to justify this activity – for example, you are testing out new equipment,or you are practising for a major expedition. Mind you, I would do it just for the hell of it. Pack a rucksack with a small tent, a few pots and pans, and a good supply of food. When you've got it all ready then you jump on a bus, tube or whatever and go off to a park or heath for a walk. (Canals are also great for this.) After a while you can settle down and cook dinner, and maybe practise putting up that tent. By the way, don't forget your waterproofs.

DEFEND THE CASTLE

This is a bit rough and tough. Divide a group into two teams, the defenders and the attackers. The 'castle' can be a high spot of land or one of those concrete play objects in the park. The rules are simple. The defenders try to stay on the castle, while the attackers try to throw them off and get on themselves. When the whole defending team is off, the attackers have won. When you are thrown off you can try to get back on, unless you were the last defender on it at the time. When a team is totally pushed off the castle, they have to go away and develop new tactics to try to get back. If anyone starts to play too roughly, they are sent off for a while to cool down.

A gentler version of this game can be played on a mat in the swimming pool.

THE ALTERNATIVE GOLF COURSE

Golf is one of those sports, like fishing, that can be hard to understand. But enthusiasts who have the bug seize any opportunity to play. Alternative golf can be played by experts or novices. You may have a few clubs and a golf ball; if not, improvise with things like broom handles or the reverse end of a snooker cue. There may be a park close by where you can practise your stroke, but you can also have a round in the house or club. Just remember that you will have to pay for any breakages – like windows, or the vase that has been in the family for years! Always look before your shot, to make sure that no one is in the way. You could have a standard club course route so that you can have competitions and compare handicaps.

GOLF FOLLOW THE LEADER

In real golf you have a course of eighteen holes and a set order of play. This game is similar, and can be played with two to five people. The course is made up as they go by the person at the front, and the order changes after a set time (say thirty minutes) so that every player has a chance to lead. The course can go anywhere, indoors or out. Each person in turn has one hit of the ball. If a player falls behind, they still have to follow the same course – if they miss out a section of the course they are out. Each player has three lives to start with and can use up a life to catch up with the rest of the group.

This game can be played completely indoors at a youth club, or outside in the park, around the flats or over local waste ground.

GOLF DISTANCE SHOOTING

For this game you need a large open area or park on a quiet day when no one is around to get hit. Make a shooting line: all players start from this, one at a time. You'll need a few markers to stick in the ground for the best shots. Each person has a set number of balls, say ten. The first player has ten shots and the furthest ball they hit is marked. The next player then has their go and tries to hit further than the other player, and their best shot is marked. This goes on until all the players have had a go. The balls are retrieved after each player's turn. The winner is the one whose ball went the furthest. You could measure this distance as a future record to beat. Between each turn, while the balls are being collected, no one is allowed to practise. This could be dangerous, as someone could get hit. All players must be behind the shooting line while another player takes their turn.

CRAZY GOLF

If you do have some old golf clubs hanging around, and there is some waste land outside, you could design and make a crazy golf course. You can use anything you find lying around, like tin cans, fallen drainpipes, pots and pans, plastic bottles to knock down, and even old plates to smash with a good shot. Have different sections for each hole and build obstacle courses which each player has to do, such as hitting a ball so that it goes over a breeze block into a plastic pipe that has been cut along its length and ends up dropping into a tin can. The larger the area, the more holes you can have. If you are having a fete or fun day to raise some funds, this would make a good sideshow.

URBAN HEAD-DRESS

If you have a look around a natural history museum, you'll see a lot of information about different cultures, past and present from all around the world. You will notice that most peoples wear some sort of headgear made out of things they find around them, such as bird feathers, bones, leather, straw or wood. Well, I think it will be a shame if in a few hundred years we city people do not have our own headgear to be remembered by. So do the same as past cultures and make your own out of what is around you: aerosol cans, plastic forks and spoons, or whatever else you can find. You could make a really colourful head-dress and wear it at special occasions.

ROPE AND ROLL

In this game you need a thick rope about 8 to 15 feet long, securely attached to a strong fixture above such as a steel girder. The rope comes down to about 4 feet above the ground. The game involves one person at a time holding the rope tightly while they stand on a dustbin, barrel, drum or anything that will roll around. When they are ready, the players roll in any direction they can, holding on to the rope for safety.

A variaton of this is to ride a BMX bike in circles with one hand on the rope, so that you can lean out from the rope without falling over.

PARK SINGING

This could be just a dare, or a serious activity to practise singing. Start with a nice open space in the park with no neighbours to upset. Remember that the public will be walking past, so if you want to get over shyness and build confidence with a few friends, this could be just the way to do it. In some Japanese schools the pupils have to stand on a busy street corner and sing out a Frank Sinatra song as loudly as possible in the rush hour – this is all to build up their confidence.

The game doesn't have to be singing; it could be reading poetry aloud, or rehearsing lines for a play. You wouldn't get me within ten miles of trying it, but I'm sure some would.

MUSICAL STAIRCASE

You need a staircase which has at least eight steps and is fairly broad. Have about six players. Each player is given an individual sound; this may be a musical note, an animal noise or the sound of something mechanical. Get all the players to stand at the top of the staircase, and as you point to them they have to step down one and make their noise. As you progress you can have them all moving up and down the stairs to make a tune of some sort. If you want to get into it even deeper, then each step down can mean a tone down of their noise, with a tone up as they step up. After a while you can change places, so that everyone has a chance to be the conductor.

BUSKING COMPETITION

I've only ever seen one busking competition - in Armagh, Northern Ireland - and I was very impressed. The competition was held on the same day as a local festival. When you enter a busking competition you are given your own patch and have to busk there at a given time to be judged. You can stay there as long as you want. The event I saw had to be musical, and there were dozens of different acts from various sections of the community, You will need to find out how your local by-laws affect busking, and pick the right area. There is a prize at the end of the day, and the busking money may be kept.

COOK-OUT

Compared with other countries where the weather is better, in Britain this is an activity very rarely tried by either young people or adults. Basically, all you are doing is cooking in the open. True, we may not have as much sunshine as the USA or Australia, but it's not that bad. Many families have a barbecue in the back garden. And, of course, people do tend to cook outside if they are camping out in the countryside or on the beach.

Cooking is a useful skill for boys and girls to learn, but a lot of the parents won't let their children near the oven. You can cook almost anywhere. You could simply have a barbecue outside the club; or go canoeing or on some other local trip with cooking gear in the boats, and stop under a bridge or on waste land, and build a fire. You may have some waste ground next to your club, so you could make a small, safe fire and use an old kettle to have a brew-up. Try baking some potatoes in silver foil. More ambitiously you could try soup of the day, toast, bacon, sausage, egg, beans, pancakes, eggy bread, and creamed rice warmed up in the opened tin for dessert - and of course a cuppa to finish. You could probably be even more inventive, with various omelettes. The whole event can be fun, can teach a survival skill and, of course, can be very tasty!

THE WEATHER

The weather is something we can't control – in fact, *it* controls *us* a lot more than we realise. We may think of weather as being good or bad, but really that depends on whether you are going out wearing your Sunday best, or you are a farmer praying for rain. In Britain we have a good mixture of weather: a little sun, rain, snow, sleet, wind and, of course, the average dull, cloudy day. Some parts of the world have the same hot, sticky and humid climate every day of the year. You can avoid the weather completely just by staying inside – or you can go out and use it.

If it is a windy day, then think of how you can use that. What can you fly in it? What vehicle can be made that is wind-powered? If it's raining, why not try to catch it, dance in it, or jump in a few puddles for the hell of it? If it's sunny, you could lie around a pool sipping a cool drink, or make a fancy sunshade hat. When it snows, there is no shortage of ideas: lots of people head for the nearest hill armed with dozens of different objects of all shapes and sizes to slide on.

We are often conditioned to fight our climate instead of accepting it and finding ways to use it. As a result, the weather can affect our moods very easily. A dull morning when young people turn up at a playground can mean a sluggish start and a lack of enthusiasm. If you want to avoid this, for example when you've had a few days of miserable weather, then a simple project of building a bonfire and brewing up a pot of water for a cup of tea will soon get things rolling – even if you do smell of smoke for the rest of the day.

If the weather is very hot or very cold, remember that the risks of heat exhaustion or hypothermia must be considered.

You can plan for a particular weather condition before it arrives, such as by making kites for the next windy day or when the weather forecast predicts windy conditions. This way you spend more time flying kites than having to make them hastily while the wind is blowing. Building sledges before it snows is a good idea too, as you can get out first on the new snow. If the weather is just too bad, or if you've had enough games in the cold and wet for the day, simply turn to the chapter on indoor activities. On the other hand, if there is a spell of fine weather, why not simply move regular club features outdoors - table tennis, the canteen and the music system?

THE GAMES

HOME-MADE SHOWER

This was a real life-saver once when we broke down in Germany on a hot day, miles away from any lakes or rivers to cool off in. We did find an old water tap near a park bench. So we collected all the cans and bottles we could find and filled them with cold water. One at a time we sat on the bench while the others stood on it, surrounded by the filled cans, and slowly poured the water over our heads. The more containers you have, the longer it lasts and the more refreshed you feel. Refill the cans after each 'shower' and let another person have a go. Ours was a very simple system; I'm sure you could make many more different sorts.

SUNBATHING PROJECT

For some, sunbathing is the most boring thing in the world, but for others it's the one thing they have being looking forward to through the winter. If you have a group that wants to get a sun tan, then get them to work together to give each other confidence to get out and bathe. This might sound silly, but some people find it embarrassing, especially if they are ultra white or they think their body isn't nice. You will be surprised how quickly a short spell at lunch-time, again in the early evening over the park or around the open-air pool, and of course at weekends, will build up a tan. You feel a lot fitter and happier for it, and you can pose in the evenings in those white tee-shirts!

RAIN DODGE

This activity is part game, part survival method. It is played along a street that is lined with tall buildings, on a day when the weather was good to begin with (and you dressed accordingly) but then it changed and it started to pour with rain. The aim is to get to your destination keeping as dry as you can, trying to run along as close to the wall as possible, dodging in and out of doorways, under shop blinds and maybe a few other people's umbrellas on the way. All the players meet at the end and see who kept the driest.

RAIN DANCE

Whereas the old Indian tribes used to dance to bring the long-awaited rains, and the Australians dance in the rain after a five-year drought – what do we do? Just moan! Well, what about following the example of that famous star Gene Kelly, who sings and dances in the rain with an umbrella just for the hell of it? The next time it's really heavy rain, you go out and jump around getting soaked just for fun, dancing and singing in the rain.

RAIN CATCHING

Imagine it's one of those days at the club base when it's pouring down outside and you have nothing planned but to stare out of the window. No problem! Get a plastic cup each and line up at the door ready to go out and catch the rain. There are different methods of playing this. One is simply to place your cup in what you think is the best position, and come back inside to watch for a set time to allow it to fill up. Another is again to have a set time – say ten minutes – in which you have to hold the cup and run around in the rain. The final idea is to strap a cup on each player's head and then all walk around outside with the rain falling into it. Each time, the winner is the one with most water in the cup. You can use a stick with measurements on it to see who has the most water, as long as the cups are all the same size; or have a measuring jug to pour the water into. If the water is brown or with bits of grit in it, disqualify the player as they have obviously scooped the water from a puddle; and no pushing others' cups over! Some players might need a change of clothes.

SNOW SLEDGING

If you have a snow-covered hill in your city, get on it and use it. It doesn't matter whether it's day or night, or whether you have the most expensive sledge on the market or a borrowed tray from the local café. You could be two or eighty-two years of age and still enjoy a ride. Snow can have many different forms, from powdery to hard and icy, and the various types of sledges perform differently according to the conditions. Some people just cannot wait to find a sledge, and soon realise they can slide down on waterproof trousers. Another crowd will turn up with black bin liners and bivy bags. They sit on them and grasp the front with two hands, then just lie back, and off they go. Cardboard is one of those materials that has hundreds of uses and, yes, sledging is one of them. It comes in the solo box size or the very large sheet designed to hold as many people as possible, where everyone piles on top of each other to slide down. If you look around the slope you will see the domestic and catering class of sledge, including all sorts of trays, dustbin lids, bread baskets, biscuit tins and washing-up bowls. Some people even pay for ready-made sledges. As long as you enjoy it, that's all that matters.

Always wear warm clothes; remember when walking back up the hill to keep to one side of the runway; and take away your rubbish and broken sledge bits afterwards.

SNOWBALL - HIGHEST AND FURTHEST

Besides needing snow, I would recommend some warm clothes that the snow will not cling to. Very simply, you make a few snowballs each and have some fun competitions to see who can throw the highest and then the furthest. I'm not sure how to measure the highest - any ideas welcome! Maybe you can use a large wall, so that when the ball hits it high up, it will leave a snow mark. Make sure there are no windows nearby.

GIANT SNOWBALL

This is another one of those snow activities that people suddenly think of as the first snow falls. All you do to start with is make a small snowball and start running it around on the snow-covered ground so that it picks up more snow. After a while it will grow so big that you will not be able to push it by yourself, so get another two or more helpers to keep it moving until it's once again too big to cope with. By then it will probably be about five or six feet tall. So what do you do with it now? Whatever you want. You could carve it, make a hole through the middle, or just leave it to see how long it stays after all the surrounding snow melts.

SNOW PERSON

I'm sure everyone has tried making a snowman - usually at the first snowfall of the year - and people never get tired of it. Well, what about having some variations, such as a snow woman, snow child, snow family, snow monster or snow cat? (I suppose a snow spider is out of the question!) If you have a group you could all go out in pairs with a theme for making snow sculptures. You could have a time limit to finish, with a nice cup of tea to look forward to. The game can be competitive or not, and the theme could be anything you like, from an object found in a bathroom to a vintage car.

SNOWBOARDING

Snowboarding has been around for at least ten years but has not yet caught on widely, even though there is a world championship. The board can be home-made. It is like a thin surfboard, about 5 feet long and made out of fibreglass or plywood; it has side fins and foot straps attached to it. The idea is to go to your local snow-covered hill and stand on the board. You then surf down the snow like a surfer would surf along a wave. Powdery snow is best, but it is possible to get some fun out of hard snow. To steer the board you lean it right to go right and left to go left: this is called carving. It is possible to jump small snow jumps. To stop you carve it towards the hill and lie back on to the hillside as it slows down. You can put up a slalom course to move in and out of poles or tin cans as you snowboard down the hill. To give you some idea of how to make a board, have a look at a professional one in a shop.

SNOW SAILBOARD

A snow sailboard is a snowboard with a sail on it. You can go down hills covered with snow, or even up them if the wind is strong enough. In fact, you do not need a hill at all; it could be a snow-covered piece of flat land or a 6-inch-deep paddling pool frozen over in the park. The sail can be a proper windsurfing sail or a home-made one based on the same idea; it needs side skegs to stop you sliding sideways. You will save a lot of time if you have a windsurfing instructor with you to show you the basics. Be careful if you make your sailboard too well, as they can travel and take off at a very fast speed. To stop or slow down, spill the wind by letting out the sail, and turn the board upwind. If you become a real expert, you could use a harness. Once again, look in a shop or magazine to see how boards are constructed, and base yours on this.

SNOW TRACKING

This is a hunting game where one or more people have to go off and either hide or keep on the move. The others have to come and look for them after a set time. The game needs settled snow, so that the hunters can follow the footprints and the one on the run can try to cover their tracks or double back to confuse the hunters so they are thrown off the track. A hunter must touch the runner for the catch; then have a new runner for the next game. You can play this in a park that has a lot of trees, or around the estates as long as there is snow.

IGLOO

Making igloos in the city – am I going mad? Not at all. Even the Eskimos are moving into cities, so I hear – so why not? When it snows, go to an area covered with snow, preferably a grassy place. Decide what size you want to make the igloo, and see how many of you there are to help – four to six will be about right.

First, you need to roll snowballs around until they get large enough to cut into bricks. The bricks can be about 2 feet by 1 foot in size. Use two people to start laying the snow bricks while the others roll more. When laying the bricks start with a circular base and build upwards, tapering in after the third level. The two builders can use bits of wood to help shape the igloo. Near the end everybody can be involved in the building. When you come to close the roof up, the snow will tend to fall in; someone will have to support it while the others build the dome over them. Alternatively, you could make the roof out of cardboard. Don't forget the entrance, otherwise the person inside will be in trouble! If it is a very snowy winter you could join up igloos to each other. Gloves are a must for this one.

GRASS SKIMBOARD

After a heavy rainfall, look for an area of flat grass which has been waterlogged. (Sounds like the local football pitch every Saturday just before the big match.) Find a piece of plywood, and you're away. Just put it on the edge of the water then walk back, take a run-up to the board and jump on to it. Hopefully you won't be face down in the mud, but rather skimming along to the other side. You could even try a windsurfer without the back skeg if there is a good wind blowing; or if you really want a laugh, try skimming on your belly or bum with some slippery waterproofs on. When the game is over, go straight to the nearest shower!

SWAMP FOOTBALL

Personally I'm not a great lover of football, as I normally end up like the lad in the film *Kez* where he climbs over the goalpost, lost in play, while the other team scores a goal. Mind you, if the conditions and rules of the game were changed a little, I might play. Some football pitches are not very well positioned and when it rains heavily, they flood. In these conditions most matches will be cancelled, but even with a foot of water on a soil or tarmac pitch, football can still be played. (A grass pitch is best left to dry out, as it would be damaged if played on when flooded.) It can be great fun running around and splashing everything in sight whilst trying to kick the ball. And you don't need to wait for a rainfall if you have a local paddling pool not being used by anyone. Put a goal at each end and start the game. Even a large puddle is enough to play in. Always check there are no hidden dangers around, such as broken glass or rocks. Some warm, dry clothes will be needed as well.

PAPER CATCH

This activity needs a windy day which is blowing the paper and other rubbish around the streets – ideally, a quiet day like a Sunday. Choose some deserted streets such as the areas around city docklands, which usually have wide roads with very little traffic. Get the whole group at the end of the street where the wind is blowing from, and each player has to pick up the same number of bits of paper rubbish off the street. On the word 'GO' everybody throws their paper into the air and then has to chase it and pick it up. You can only pick up your own rubbish – the way to tell if it is yours is to tear a shape on each piece of paper beforehand. The first with all their papers shouts out and has them checked to see that they all have the right marks. This goes on for second place, third and so on until all the bits have been caught. They are then placed into the bin – so not only have you had fun, you have cleaned up the street a little.

Another way to play this game is simply to have a set time starting at one end of the street, and grab as many pieces of paper flying around in that time, and count them at the end to see who has the most.

BALL WIND RACE

This game can be played on water or on land, but both need a fair wind blowing and you need some balls of similar size. If the game is on water you need to stand downwind at the edge of the lake or pond, each with a ball. Throw one ball as far out over the water as you can, then the others have to throw their balls as close to the first one as possible. If they are not close, it is a fail throw and they must throw again. Because the wind is blowing towards you, the balls will be blown back to the bank. The winner can be either the player whose ball gets to the bank first, or the one who is last. If last, this may

eliminate the cheaters as you will then throw the ball out as far as possible. If you have a swimming pool or a small pond outside then you can all line up upwind and place the balls in a line on the water; as they blow across, you walk around to collect the winner. The balls must touch the bank to finish; no reaching out, as you may fall in.

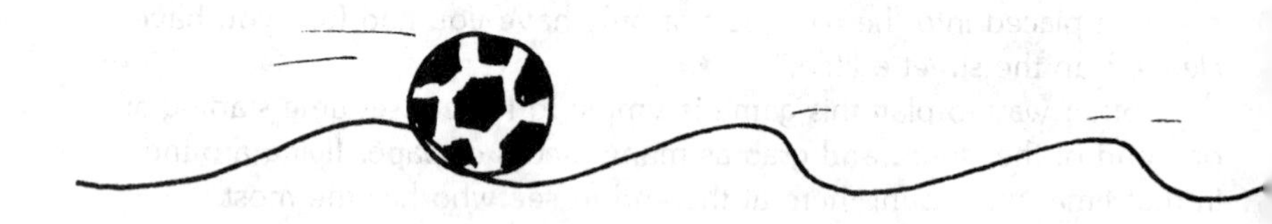

If you don't have water at all, then a large playground will do if it is flat and windy. In an area with lots of buildings around there may be strange winds that bounce off the buildings and blow the balls all over the playground, which may add interest. No touching the balls.

BODY KITE

When it's one of those days when the winds are about 40 mph and most activities are a blow-out, why not put your coats on and all go outside into the full force of the wind and try to make a stand against it – if you dare! Face the wind and open your coat, holding the bottom corners. Open the coat out like wings and catch the wind; try not to get pushed back. Keep your feet still and see how far you can lean into the wind without falling over. Try it with lots of people all in a line with linked arms and holding their coats, trying to lean into the wind. If you survive that, then lift the corners of the coat above your head so it's like a high sail. Mind those sudden gusts, or you'll be on the grass!

SHADOW JUMPING

This game is best when the sun is either coming up or going down, so that the shadows are cast long across the pavement as cars drive past. The idea is that a shadow is deadly, and the only way to stay alive is to jump over it. (Life becomes very difficult when a long lorry comes along.) You can stay on one spot and let the cars go past, or walk along on the way to wherever you are going. If you get hit by a shadow five times, you're out. You must always stay on the pavement for safety.

SHADOW TREADING OR DODGING

The aim in this game is to get from one part of your estate to another, or from one street to another a mile away, treading only on shadows or patches of sunlight, whichever you decide. This includes shadows made by passing people, cars or anything else. For example, if you are only allowed on the shadows, which are usually made by parked cars, and there is a gap of light too big to jump, you may have to go back a bit to the shadow of a lamp-post so that you can walk across to another section of shadows. If you are on the sunlight and a person walks past, you have to jump over their shadow. If you have a long journey, take some watches with alarms that you can set to go off every two minutes. This will mean a change from walking on the shadows to sticking to the light bits, and vice versa, until you reach your destination. If you are playing on the street, you are only allowed to cross the road at the traffic lights or crossing.

WASHING CLOTHES

This doesn't sound like much fun to most people, but it's a skill that young people rarely learn until they get their own place. I don't mean running the dirty clothes down to the launderette, but washing them by hand and letting the sun dry them out. You can try it if you are going to a camp for a couple of weeks, or incorportate it in part of an award scheme. You may just need some stuff washed at the club - make a group activity out of it.

PUDDLE CROSSING

After a heavy rainfall you can often find a large puddle around the flats and streets, especially if the drains have been blocked up with leaves. Have a look around for some old bricks, stones and planks. The task is to cross the widest part of the puddle without getting your feet wet. You could build a bridge so you can walk over, or work out a method using a few bricks so that you can stand on two while you move another in front of you; this goes on until you get to the other side. You could make a bridge wide enough to ride your push-bike or go-kart over, or you could even go across on roller skates!

PUDDLE JUMPING

Imagine one of those rainy days when it seems as if it will never stop. You want to get out of the house, but can't think what to do. Well, now your problem is solved. Get some friends together and make sure you all have old clothes on. Psych each other up and then get out and

jump in every puddle you can find as many times as you can. If you find any mud, you might as well jump in that as well. If the group is young, make sure their parents know they are going get dirty. If you don't do this, you had better hide for at least a month! (I've written this for the adults, as young children will play this game anyway, with or without their parents' knowledge.)

NIGHT ACTIVITIES

A familiar area during the day can seem very different at night. The night has its own characteristics which change with the seasons. In the day-time a city centre may be packed with people rushing to and from their offices, bustle, shoppers and traffic; but at night you're lucky to find anyone there. Parks like Central Park in New York or Hampstead Heath in London can be full of life during the day, with families and children happily playing around, but when it's dark, few people dare to cross them.

The night has its own rhythm. In the evening, people rush to get home from work. Then, after a short while, they come out to hit the town, and about midnight you see bleary-eyed people stumbling home, yawning. After that, it goes very quiet for a few hours. This is a really nice time to walk around in the silence. You might come across the odd bunch of homeless people with a little fire on the go to keep them warm. If you've been working late, it's nice to drive around and find a night tea stand; a cuppa and a bacon sandwich taste better outside in the cold night air. Then the early-morning workers arrive. Meat, fish and vegetables are all loaded into vans before dawn, for the coming day's trading.

Most of us live by day and sleep by night, so it can be something really special for a young person to be out very late. The dark is exciting for some, and scary for others. Sometimes, just being allowed out by their parents is enough for youngsters to enjoy a night adventure. Of couse, other young people have nowhere else to be but outside, so the night does have its own sadness as well.

A game of run-outs, or a canoe along the canal, is totally different played in the dark. To me, noises always seem more noticeable during the night. You don't need to be out on the street to have an adventure: you could simply sleep at the club, as a group activity. Sometimes, things you would enjoy and experience naturally living in the countryside are missed in the cities. For example, when did you last watch a sunrise?

The night can be a very private time, when you have the opportunity to think for a while. It's very rare to be in complete darkness in a city. That's why it's so interesting when there is a power cut. You have different experiences, you see how people cope - but, you can miss your dinner.

For years I was scared of the dark, although it didn't stop me playing in it. With some friends I ran away from home and decided to live in a local derelict house. We had played in it for years during the day, and knew every missing floorboard and smashed window. But as the night crept in we started to be a little scared, so we ran into the street and borrowed a couple of red road lights off a skip and brought them back to light up our room (not recommended!) After a while the ghost stories started to come to mind. We all decided we were homesick, and rushed away.

Christmas is a great time to get out of the club and walk through the lit streets just looking at shops. All sorts of activities which you wouldn't have thought possible can be played in the dark, such as basketball or football by candlelight - a torch on each goal. Orienteering can sound boring to young people, but if you plan it for night-time and call it by a different name, like 'Cops and Robbers', you will be inundated with members wanting to play.

Safety is a vital consideration, what with bumping into things in the dark, and meeting undesirable people walking around. You *must* get permission from parents if the group is young. If the activity is on the streets, you should stay in small groups with at least one responsible person in each. Carry a contact phone number: if you get lost or need help, at the other end off the phone there is a helper with a car to come and get you. A note for the police may also be useful, to let them know what's going on.

There's not much new to say about the inevitable discos, but you can make them more interesting. Perhaps you could have mini discos every Friday night for your own members, have a big one inviting friendly local clubs, or let your members bring friends once a month. You could have different theme discos, or roller-skating discos, or even a roof disco if the roof is safe and suitable, i.e. fenced like some school roof playgrounds.

If all this seems too much, why not just sit down and watch day turn to night? If you're near a park, this change will be more obvious: all sorts of animals and insects appear, and people's noises and activities alter at this time.

The night has its own dangers, but it's up to the organisers' common sense to cope with these challenges. Night activities are worth the effort, and can be a great maturing and learning process for the individuals taking part. They will talk about their adventures for years to come!

THE GAMES

STAR WATCH

If you have a very clear, dark night with millions of stars visible, find a nice, dry, quiet place to lie on your back and stare into space. I often do this for half an hour when I sleep out. You will be surprised what you will see shoot past although your mind does start going on a wander after a while. This activity is best done away from street lights, as you will see more in total darkness. You could even stay up in a small group with a couple of telescopes. It amazes me that most people watch more space on TV than for real, when they need only look through the window.

SLEEPING UNDER THE STARS

It's amazing how many people have never slept out in the open under the stars for the whole night. You should have some plastic under you to stop the damp, as even in a heatwave the damp will rise at night. You still use a sleeping bag, and maybe a woollen hat. Pick the site so that you are not in any danger – possibly at the back of your club, or on the green in the middle of the estate. You could share a flask of warm milk and tell each other stories before you go to sleep.

CHINESE LANTERNS

This activity comes from an old Chinese custom when someone has died, and it is very simple and beautiful. It is done at night, near water, during a barbecue or party. To make the lanterns, you need dozens of those small paper cake cases and the same number of birthday-type candles. Make them up a few hours before you need them, fixing a candle in each cup by lighting the candle and allowing the wax to drip into the cup so you can stand the candle upright. Then blow the candles out, ready for later. Make as many as you can and place them on trays: a good number would be about forty. At the right time during the party, light the candles and place them carefully on the water. For safety reasons you can only do this when there is little or no wind, otherwise they will get blown out of sight and become a fire risk. If conditions are right, the lights should drift slowly around in front of you for about twenty minutes, illuminating the water beautifully.

TIN-CAN LANTERNS

This is a night game – the darker the better. Have a look around for some old tin cans. You also need a can opener and some candles. Each person has to make a lantern out of a tin by opening up the side with the can opener and placing a candle inside. You can tie a stick of wood on to one end of the can so that you can hold it in front of you. When you have all made your lanterns, and have remembered to bring the matches, you can light them up and go for a walk with the lanterns lighting the way.

COPS AND ROBBERS

This is quite a big game and needs organising well so that it runs smoothly. The game starts at twelve midnight and finishes at five o'clock the next morning. You need three staff with a car each to be the 'cops', and a group of about thirty to be the 'robbers'. The robbers split up into groups of about five with one older, responsible person in each group for safety. Every group has an emergency phone number, with a vehicle and driver on hand to rescue anyone in trouble or tired.

The groups set off at ten minute intervals and they have five hours to get all the answers to a list of questions they have been given along with a map. A line drawn on the map shows them the area they have to stay in. The questions have been worked out days before, and would be something like: what is the name of the ship moored in between two named bridges? or: how many lamp-posts are there in a certain street in the West End? or even: find out what is written in The Hilton Hotel over the reception desk. There should be about fifty questions that have to be solved within a given area of about five square miles.

The problem comes when you have got a few points, and then one of the cops jumps out on you and takes away ten points as a fine for being caught. Then the cop lets you go on your way to continue getting points, and you try not to get caught again! Every team has to be back at the club at a given time and with a full team, otherwise they lose all their points.

Have some prizes for winners and some bread and soup for everybody, and perhaps a few sleeping bags for anyone too tired to go straight home. It sounds a lot of work, but everyone gets into it and has a really good night. Each group should carry a note in case the police stop them and ask what is going on.

NIGHT ADVENTURE TASKS

The ideal area for this event would be a part of the city which includes a canal or stream, a wall to abseil down, a pool, a field and a low bridge. The more things around to use the better. The activity can be either an inter-club do, or just for your own club. The game is played at night to add a bit of spice, and it should be well planned beforehand.

Basically, you set up lots of locations around a given area of a couple of square miles, each containing one task to do. Divide the people into small groups and give them a map of the set route to follow. The teams can set off at different times, or they can all go at the same time with a different order of tasks to follow. The aim is to complete all the tasks in the fastest time. Each location will have a suitable person supervising it, for two reasons: firstly for safety – someone who knows exactly what is going on during that task; and secondly to check who has completed the task properly. If there are lots of clubs playing, then each club can be responsible for setting up one task and making sure that there are people to look after that event. The following are a few ideas.

1 Abseil down a wall or out of the club window.
2 Make a raft to cross the canal or river.
3 Swim a given distance taking a floating object with you.
4 Rope crawl across a stream or mud pit.
5 Hop the length of the street.
6 Eat six doughnuts.

The groups have to stay in their teams and they have a contact number in case of trouble. The game has a set time limit. Each group should carry a letter from the club explaining what they are doing, and it would be a good idea to tell the local police beforehand so they know what to expect. Any dangerous activities must be covered by an instructor in that field, and there should be a couple of cars with drivers available in case of any problems that might arise.

BLACKOUT

Some people in the cities have never experienced total darkness; normally, even in a dark street or room, there is always some flicker of light. The idea is to find a place or a room that has no light at all. This should not be too small, and you should not be able to see your hand in front of you. When you find such a place, and have made sure that there are no dangers in it like poles to bump your head on,etc., put a group in there and let them mill around. You can have different themes such as no speaking, or constant screaming, which must start when ordered. One game would be for one player to hold an object while everyone else has to try to find it. When someone does get it, it is their turn to carry it around, avoiding the others in the dark.

GAMES IN THE DARK

This idea came from a group I was watching playing basketball as the sun was setting. I thought I might as well stay and see the end of the game and a nice sunset. I saw the sunset, but the game went on for ages, well into the evening. The village had no electric lights, but they carried on playing in the dark – and even got a few goals.

How about playing football or basketball indoors in the dark, with only one tiny light on each goal? You could try it in total darkness, but I'm not sure that you could trust the players to tell you whether or not they had scored a goal. You will need to calm the players down now and again if they kick or throw the ball too hard. Usually, at any club there is always someone who will turn off the light while you are playing. I'll bet the same smart alec tries to turn them on in this one.

NIGHT FACE PAINT

One variation on a night game where different teams have to creep around to surprise each other is that in which all players have to make up their faces like warpainted tribesmen, with a night-glowing paint. No one is allowed to cover up their faces as they move around. Make sure the paint is suitable for skin use – maybe ask in a trendy fashion store or theatrical make-up shop.

GLOW-WORMS

What I call 'glow-worms' (besides the real thing) are those sticks of about 8 inches in length which when broken glow bright green. You can buy them in camping shops, and they glow for hours. These can be used for many different activities at night: you can stick them on your push-bike, canoe or go-kart as a pretty light, or if you hide a few you could have a glowing treasure hunt, positioning them with just a little bit showing under a brick or up a tree.

You could have a type of hunt game where one person has a glow-worm attached to their body, which they are not allowed to take off or cover, and they have to run off and hide from the rest. The others, after a few minutes, go in search of the glow-worm. The runner must not stay hidden for more than five minutes in any one hiding place. This game is well suited to large estates or clubs. When the runner is caught, the catcher then wears the glow-worm and the game continues.

COMMANDO CREEPING

This is a great game. You play it at night, dress in dark clothes, and put mud on your face if you are white-skinned. The idea is to creep around the grounds of your estate or park pretending to be commandos, as if you have just landed and don't want anyone to see you. You could divide into two teams and try to spot each other. It is quite a skill not to be seen or heard, and for some even smelt!

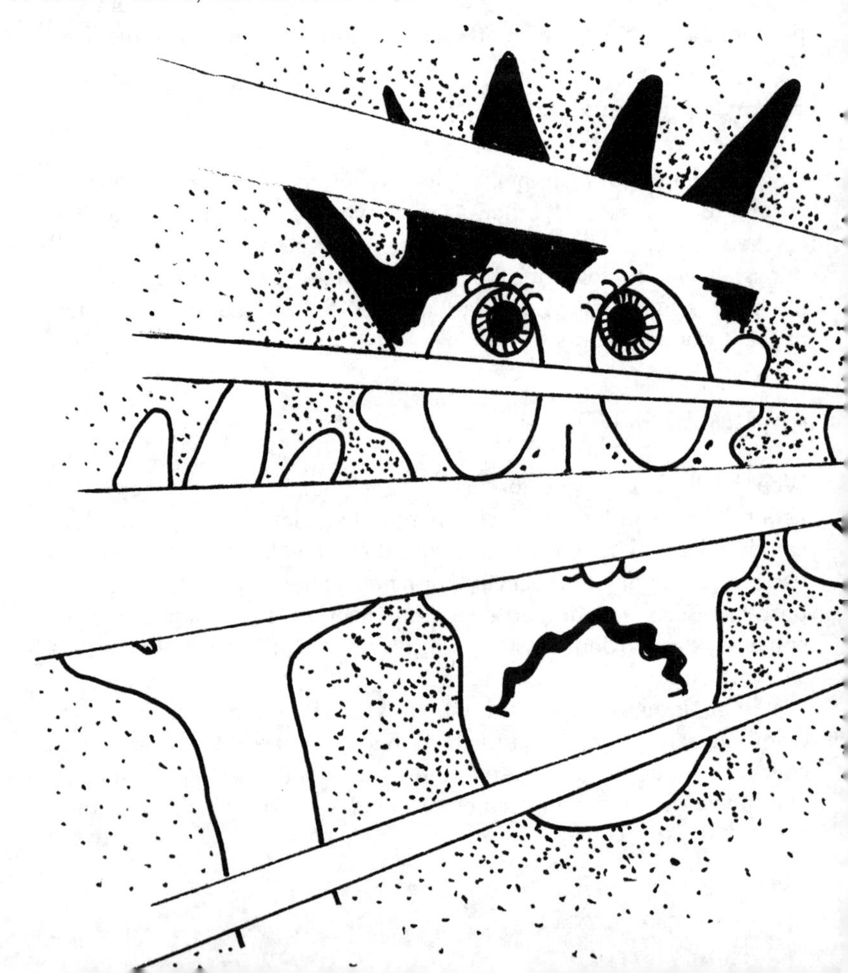

TORCH BEAM KILLER

This game is played in the dark and can be indoors in a large club building or around the flats on a dark night, or even in the park. The only equipment needed is a torch each. First you decide on an area to play in, which you must not go out of. Have a whistle to bring everybody back to a set meeting place for the half-way change-over point, the end of the game or in an emergency. You can split the group up into two halves or have a hit squad of four people. One side or group runs off and tries to keep out of sight, and after a short time the others come after them with torches. The hunters creep around without using the torches so that in the dark the runners aren't sure if they are their own group or not. To catch or kill a person you suddenly shine the light in their eyes and say 'you're dead'. When you have been caught, you have to go back to the start where there will be a light shining on you all the time. When everyone is caught, or after a given time, you change roles. Players must always stay in pairs for safety, whether they are hunters or runners. Remember, the emergency whistle means return right away.

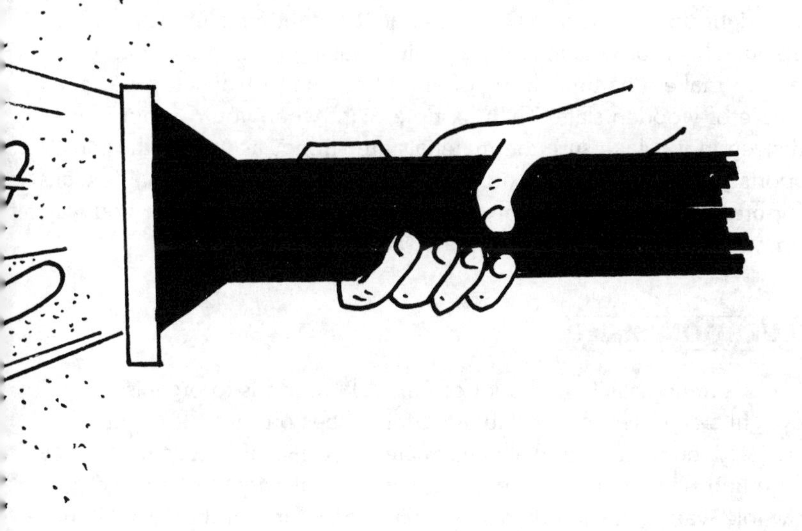

WHISTLE CODE

In some countries the police use whistles to transmit different messages to each other. This game is based on that idea. Divide the group into two teams, each equipped with a whistle. Each team then invents its own whistle code, without letting the other team know what it is. After 10–15 minutes of conferring, get both teams back together and set each a task to do against the other, such as steal a ball which is hidden in their secret camp. You need to have one whistle code which everyone knows, to bring the teams back together in case of emergency or to start a new game. The team whistle codes can be used to pinpoint the other team's camp, or to warn that the enemy is near. You may also have some decoys worked out.

You can play this in housing estates or in the park at night – in fact, in any large, dark area. But if you do play it in built-up areas, I wouldn't do it too often, because of the noise.

HAMMOCK NIGHT OUT

This is right up my street, as I like any activity that ends up with sleeping. This project is in two parts: first making it, then using it. The idea is to make a hammock out of an old curtain or blanket, rope, and a couple of wooden slats. Then fix up a night when you can put it up and sleep in it. Make sure the materials are strong, as well as the supports you tie them up to (not too high!) Don't forget to get a few bits in for breakfast. The better you make the hammock, the better you will sleep.

CLUBROOM SLEEP

This is a simple activity and a lot of fun. All you do is to organise a one-night sleep-over in the club in sleeping bags on mats. It might sound silly, but it can be really enjoyable, especially if everyone can stay up late and have a ghost story and a few bags of crisps. You could go the whole way by having dinner, sleeping together and then waking up to make breakfast. If young people did this at home they *would* be bored, but to do it at the club with a few friends is a real adventure.

SOLO CAMP

This is for maturing young people, and for some it can be a very hard thing to do. The idea is that each individual must camp out for the night by themselves with a tent or bivy. You need to know the participants and to organise it so that the risks are cut down to a minimum. It might sound pretty terrifying with so many disturbed people around, but there *are* ways to run it safely. One way would be to have a small group that splits up to camp by themselves within an appropriate area. They don't know it, but you will be awake and patrolling the area all night. In the morning you all meet at a given time and place for breakfast. Each person should carry a whistle. Take care that your creeping around is not heard by them, as sound carries a long way at night and they might be scared enough by all the natural noises around them. Some will try to meet each other for a party, so arrange them carefully and search them for alcoholic drink. A private letter to parents to explain the safety cover might be useful, with the emphasis on the value of such an exercise.

HOME-MADE BED

This is another game sleeping out in the open in a safe place. This time you can't use your sleeping bag or bed sheets; you have to make your own bed out of newpapers, polythene and other junk. You could say that it's a bit like being a tramp; some of those tramps are real experts on thermal rubbish!

NIGHT POOL PARTY

If you have a local swimming pool, especially one of the modern ones with wave machines and slides, you could apply for permission for a special one-off use of the pool starting at midnight and going on until whatever time you decide. You can take music with you and have a mini-bus outside to take people home afterwards. Of course, you need to have a good relationship with the pool manager, and to make sure that there are lifeguards at the pool-side. Given that, there is no reason that you shouldn't get permission, and I have certainly known it to happen.

CLIMBING WALL NIGHT OUT

If you have one of those climbing walls near your club, or have a wall you can use safely, try climbing half-way up it as though you are scaling Everest and have to camp for the night. Professional climbers can show you the methods and equipment to use. The aim is to try to get as comfortable as possible and see if you can sleep there all night. After all, you never know when you will need to sleep on a mountain face, do you? You need an instructor to supervise this one.

STAYING AWAKE ALL NIGHT

Have you ever tried to stay up all night so that you see the sun go down and then come up again the next day? Some people who fish all night experience this. You could move the tables and soft chairs outside the clubroom into the open, put the radio on low, get the hot chocolate on the boil and play some cards or other games. You could even turn the radio off and talk about life, or simply meditate. After (if) the sun does come up, you can then go home and sleep.

SPECIAL EQUIPMENT

It's hard to define special equipment in detail, because it varies so much. I think the closest I can get would be to say that it is equipment that is professionally made and usually bought from the shops. You may already have some at home, accumulated over the years. It can range from tiddlywinks, push-bikes or hockey sticks to skis, canoes and climbing equipment. Some of these things can obviously be used without supervision, but when it comes to equipment like canoes and climbing gear, a responsible person with experience in that particular sport, and if possible an instructor, must be in charge.

Equipment should be suitable for the task and in good working condition. It should be checked regularly for faults and wear and tear. Some equipment is too expensive for individuals to buy, but a club or your local council may have a store for the community to use – for example canoes, bikes, tents, sleeping bags and cookery equipment for camping. I know of one council that even has skis.

Any time you are using equipment, make sure you have permission, and that the area is safe. For example, if you're using bikes or skateboards, check for broken glass on the ground. The instructor is responsible for the group's safety, and they should also know about insurance cover for the group and third parties. Risky sports must have parental permission if under-age membes are involved. The activities in this chapter can be exciting and useful for learning skills. They can also be lots of fun, used in displays or as part of sponsored events.

You don't have to use equipment for its original purpose, if you can find another use which is safe and doesn't damage it. And you don't have to use equipment on its own – you may wish to combine different sorts of gear. For example, roller skates and hockey sticks together, or skateboards and basketball.

One area I know has a centre for the unemployed that uses push-bikes in many different ways. Because of the expense and lack of public transport they got a fleet of push-bikes. Not only does this provide an outdoor activity where they can ride off into the countryside, it also allows them to move around town cheaply, perhaps to look for jobs.

Simply putting up a tent on some waste land can be fun and good experience for the group if they want to camp further afield. Activities with equipment are endless in terms of what you can do, what you can use, what you can learn, what you can see, and the amount of fun you can have!

THE GAMES

FOOT DOWN

Foot down is played on push bikes in a confined area such as inside a large hall or outside in a fenced area for football. Every player needs a two-wheeled bike; no three-wheelers, although any monocycle riders will be most welcome. Players cycle around the confined area with the aim of getting the others to put their feet down. This doesn't mean one big push to send them crashing to the floor, but more subtle tactics and skilful cycling. One technique could be stopping in front of another player for a couple of seconds and then moving on – they will be out if they put their feet down. When you are out you have to stand by the wall for two minutes and then you can return. The last person to be still on a bike when all the others are at the wall is the winner.

THE BIVY BAG

To those people who do not know what a bivy bag is, well it's a large, normally bright orange polythene bag that comes in two main sizes: 6 feet by 3 feet, and a larger group bag size that very many people can get inside. They are used in an emergency when someone gets very cold and needs to cut down heat loss. Mind you, they can be used in lots of other ways:

1 Bivy bag race: like a sack race where you stand inside it and hop along.
2 Bivy bag camp. A group of you sleep out the night in a bivy bag.

3 Bivy bag as a sledge on snow.
4 Blow-up-the-bivy-bag-race. You need to fill the bag up with air to make it as large as possible, and if it is an old one you can burst it afterwards. Do not try to fill the bag up by blowing from your lungs, as you may hyperventilate and become unconscious. Run along and capture the air instead, or use a foot pump.
5 Bivy bag walkabout. With one of the large group bivy bags, get as many people in it as possible with them all standing up so that the bag is over their heads and they cannot see. One person stays on the outside for safety to make sure they don't fall down anywhere dangerous. The idea is to walk about trying to get from one place or room to another. It can be played inside or out. The watcher only speaks if there is real danger – not just a little bump into the wall.

Use old bags, not ones you may need in an emergency later on.

CLIMBING WALL FOLLOW THE LEADER

When you have a group using the climbing wall and they have warmed up and had some time to get to know the wall, you can play follow the leader to improve their skills a bit more. If it is a long, corridor-type wall, they can all follow close behind. If it is a vertical wall there will have to be a larger gap so they don't tread on others' fingers or fall on each other. If it is a high wall where you need ropes, you will have to plot a course and try it one by one. Different sections of the wall can be done with one arm behind their back, or you could make a rule that some holes and bumps cannot be used. Whatever you do, it must be OK with the instructor. You must always have an instructor with this specialist equipment.

PRUSICKING

Prusicking is another fun activity, but it can be very tiring. It is almost the opposite to abseiling where you slide down ropes: here, you go up them, although not so fast. You do need an instructor, and good conditions and equipment. Basically you have a rope and two special hand clamps that have string foot-rests on them which you move in turn to go up the rope. This can be done inside or out; high up or only 10 feet off the ground to the first landing. You could combine a prusic up and an abseil down, or the whole thing could be one part of an obstacle course. Find a local expert for more information.

ABSEILING

Abseiling is great fun and a big challenge for the first few times. It sounds as if you need a lot of wind, but in fact it has nothing to do with boats but means sliding down ropes from heights. This is a specialist activity and will need a suitable instructor with equipment in good order. In most cities you can find some climbers or a group to give you a go. This can be done indoors and out. I do not want to go into detail here on how to set the whole thing up and safety points, as the instructor will cover all this. A few fun sessions may include the following: abseiling with equipment from different heights indoors and out; different methods of locking off; getting into projects such as transporting equipment down; stopping half-way to take photos; practising first aid on a partner on a rope next to you. Have fun, but always do it with an expert.

SLAVE ROPE CHAIN

This can be played indoors or out; all you need is a long rope of the climbing type that is getting old and is not going to be used for climbing any more. About ten or more can play. You need to attach the rope around your waists so you are all spaced out along its length. The knot should not be a slip knot, as this might hurt the player. When you are all on the rope you play follow the leader, climbing under tables and out of ground-floor windows looking for safe adventures. Stay away from roads, and never put the rope round a player's neck.

FOOTBALL LINE TAG

Even if you don't like the game of football, you can still use the pitch for a game of line tag. Lots of people can play. Every player must stand on one of the lines marking out the pitch, goal and penalty areas. You must not step off these lines or you are out. One person is 'on' and has to transfer their 'tag' to another player by running along the lines. If there is no football pitch or other game field available, you can draw chalk lines on the tarmac to your own design. The school P.E. halls with 3 or 4 different pitches marked on top of each other would be perfect for this.

SKATEBOARDS

Try to arrange a skateboard trip in which everyone has their own board and you all go off to an area with lots of slopes. If you have only a few skateboards, you can share. You could even try to make your own – it's hard to get it to steer well but you can make a specialist one for speed which is about 5 feet long with the wheels at the ends. You lie down on your back with this one to cut down wind resistance. If a slope is too steep, or you are like me and not very good at it, you can sit on the board rather than stand. There may be some experts in your club, and you could rig up some ramps and a half-pipe for them to perform on. If you only have a flat playground you could use tin cans to make a slalom course, and perhaps put a sail on the board to use the wind. You could make a triple board or an extra wide one for beginners. Have a first-aid kit, as someone is bound to get a graze.

TYROLEAN ROPE CRAWL

The task is to stretch a rope across an area so that people can hold on to it with their feet and hands and slide along it. The rope should not be so high that if someone fell off they would hurt themselves. The rope will sag in the middle, so make it as taut as possible. Use gloves if you do not have hard hands, and if you like, use a climbing harness. One idea is to cross over water from one bank to the other. Try transporting equipment across, such as a canoe or rucksack that is also tied on the rope and you can slide across with you. Make sure that the knots at the ends of the rope are absolutely secure. Get an experienced climber to advise you.

BMX TAG

A BMX is a push-bike with short wheels, a strong frame, wide handlebars and tyres with good grips. They are very strong, good turners and can go over obstacles and rough ground. This game can be played around the estates, over the park or on waste land. All the players in the group are on their bikes, and one or two people are 'on'. Their job is to catch and tag the others. To tag someone can be simply to touch them, or if everyone has a bit of rag sticking out of their teeshirt it has to be snatched so that person then becomes 'on'. Decide before the game starts whether you want one person on by themselves or prefer to let the tagged players become more catchers. The last one caught is the winner. The first person who was caught is on in the next game. For added interest you could play this on waste land or on muddy ground. Keep away from traffic, as your mind will be on the game and not on passing cars; and wear gloves and helmet for protection, as you could fall off a few times.

OBJECT CARRIERS

This game can be used in a fun situation or in a real domestic problem where you move a heavy object from one place to another. The idea is to use objects like roller skates, skateboards, bikes and prams arranged in the best way to transport something. This could be a game, for example, where all the players have a foot on one roller skate and a bucket of water on the other skate and have to race over a set course; or you could lash two bikes together to rest a long pipe on them to transport it down the road. So the next time the club fridge has to be moved, you won't need to break your back if there are two or three skateboards around to do the trick.

POLO ON WHEELS

Polo looks great fun on horseback, but that's more of a game for the aristocrats who have plenty of horses available. Nevertheless we can still enjoy a form of the sport by getting some sticks to use to hit the ball or puck, and using various vehicles such as push bikes, skates, skateboards and even wheelchairs. The aim is simply to get the object into the opposite team's goal. A word of advice: wrap up your ankles for protection.

HOSEPIPE FIGHT

It's been one of those really hot summer days which we are always dreaming about and when it comes we feel knocked out and wish it was cooler so we had the energy to do something! Well, it only takes one person to connect the hosepipe and give everybody a surprise soaking. After the initial shock, you can all mess around playing with the water.

SKATEBOARD BASKETBALL

Not a lot to write about this game, as the title explains it very well. You play a game of basketball with normal rules, the only difference being that each player is on a skateboard. In basketball you can only move so many steps with the ball; on the skateboard, you can push the ball along the same number of times. It might be a good idea to wear some pads on your elbow and knee joints.

SKATE SCOOTING

This game originally started because of a shortage of roller skates. Say there are ten people but only five pairs of skates: each player therefore has one skate. You put the skate on one foot and push yourself along with the other. You can play races, run-outs or any other chasing type of game. You could even go on a journey round the estate.

SHOVEL HOPPING

This is a very skilful activity often played around building sites when club members are bored. It makes shovelling about fifty times harder, but a lot more fun. Get as many shovels as possible and give one to each player. You simply hold the handle with both hands and step up on the blade like a pogo stick. Then you hop all around, seeing how long you can stay up or how far you can travel. This game is not a good idea indoors!

WHEELBARROW RACE

This is another building-site pastime where you get as many wheelbarrows with large air-inflated tyres as possible and line up together ready to race. On the command 'GO' you lever the barrow up with your knees while holding the handles so that it bounces. Then you race forward, keeping the barrow bouncing as high as possible. When you have mastered this you can have an obstacle course made out of bricks and other found bits and pieces that you have to bounce over.

PARACHUTE FOOTBALL

This game is for very large groups of up to about two hundred; you need an extra-large parachute, or two joined together. Simply lay the chute out on the ground with the kids all the way around the edge holding it with both hands. Divide the group into teams: if it's a round chute divide them up into four, or if it is square then each side is a team. Get them to hold the chute at waist height and lift their arms up and down. Meanwhile, throw a ball in the middle; it will bounce and roll all over the place. The idea is to bounce the ball over the heads of another team; when that happens they get a penalty point. The first team to get three points loses and a new game starts. If the ball isn't getting enough bounce, get the players to move back and tighten the chute, then it will go better.

PARACHUTE TRAP

Using a parachute that has all its strings cut away, get the players to open the chute and stand around it, holding the edge with two hands. The idea is that the players hold the chute close to the ground then all stand up and hold it as high above their heads as possible - then down again. This goes on up and down until the leader calls a particular group of players who then have to let go of the chute as it is going up, run under it and try to get to the other side. Meanwhile, the others still holding the chute have to try to trap those under it by pressing it to the ground so they can't get out. After a while you let the trapped players out and start again, but this time the leader picks a different group. Here are a few ideas for groups: players wearing anything red, black shoes, boys, girls, etc. Keep an ear open in case you hear a younger child getting scared underneath the chute.

PARACHUTE SHARKS

Get a group of fifty to a hundred around a chute with its strings cut away. They hold the chute with two hands, all spread out around it. One person is picked to be a 'shark' and has to get under the chute with their hands together above their heads so that it looks like a shark's fin from above. The shark has to try to get to the edge of the chute and grab someone's leg or arm and drag them underneath as well. The victim becomes another shark, and they carry on trying to grab victims. Sharks must stay under the chute at all times. The others try to stop getting grabbed by pressing the chute down to the ground as the shark comes their way. If the sharks are not too close you can provoke them by lifting your part of the chute. When does the game end? That depends on the sharks' appetite!

PARACHUTE HIDE-UNDER

Lay out a parachute flat on the ground for a very young group so they can crawl over and under it at will. You could put a few tables and chairs under it to add to the excitement by making it into a camp. Try propping up a large chute with a few poles to make a small version of a circus big top, and then let the kids loose in it. If you can't get a parachute from your local army surplus store, you could use a large sheet – but the number of players will have to be smaller.

TEACH A SKILL

If you're a teacher or an instructor of some sort and you have been working within a group for a while, then how about letting them loose on their own? Say, for example, you have been teaching a sport like boardsailing and the group has reached a proficient standard, then divide them into pairs. One partner becomes the teacher and the other has to be the student. The teaching partner has to coach the student in one particular skill in the sport, and then they change places and the other partner has a go at teaching. This can turn out to be either a useful experience or a real disaster area, so be prepared. You will need to move around to make sure no bad techniques are being taught, and you may help a little here and there.

BROOM FOOTBALL

This is played to the same rules as normal football British style, but instead of your feet you use brooms. The biggest problem is finding enough brooms to play with. If you are playing indoors soft brooms are best, but if you are playing on a dusty pitch outside you need to use the hard, bristly type otherwise you will destroy them and never be able to return them to their rightful owners. A normal ball is used, and five-a-side is probably best.

SPOTTING

Some people love to spot things, while for others it's hard to understand the excitement gained from this activity. It's a bit like fishing or golf: if you are not into it, you can't understand why people spend so many hours in all sorts of weather doing it. The city is full of things to spot, from trains and car number plates to double-decker buses. The idea, for example, could be to collect the numbers of as many trains as possible in a particular class. (I'm not sure what you do with them when you have them!) I think it's almost a sort of drug, as once you start it's hard to stop. One idea is to identify some of the planes that fly over your city. If you have some binoculars or a telescope, you can clearly make out what airline or what country a plane belongs to from its markings. If you have a book on planes, you may be able to identify the model and class of the plane as well.

PLAYGROUND HIGHLAND GAMES

We often have athletics meetings or play rounders etc. in playgrounds. Well, why not have a change and hold a Highland Games where you can make some some simplified fun versions of the events normally held in the games, such as tossing the caber or ball and chain throwing? These could be in miniature for younger people, and some of the running events can be silly three-legged ones. You could even make cabers out of foam, and have a few wet sponge throwing events. In the background you could play some Scottish bagpipe music to give atmosphere, and instead of a hot-dog stand for eats you could sell haggis and shortbread.

A DAY'S SUPPLY

In this activity the idea is that one evening you have to make up a package of supplies of food and drink to last you the whole of the next day. You need to cover everything you will need to eat and drink during the day, because you are not allowed to spend any money at all, nor even get water from a tap. If anyone offers you something, you have to refuse it. The idea is to carry your supplies around with you from the time you wake up until you go to bed. You may be going out for the day, or just going about your normal routine. Remember to tell your family so that you don't end up with a meal prepared for you, as this will either go to waste or prove too much of a temptation to resist. Trips with the group are a good time to try this, as you can keep an eye on each other. How about doing it for a whole weekend?

TIME BOMB

Keep your hair on – it's not a real bomb, only an alarm clock! The game is played on an old piece of waste land with all sorts of rubbish lying around. You have an alarm clock fully wound up with the alarm set to go off in, say, ten or twenty minutes. The group close their eyes while one member goes off and hides the clock, or time bomb. The others, when told to start, then have a set time to find the bomb before it goes off. The person who finds it has to hide it for the next game; if it is not found, the person who hid it first can hide it again. There are many places where you could play this game, for example in the wooded area of a park or inside the club building.

ON THE STREET

Every city consists mostly of streets. These can vary from red mosaic bricks laid in lovely patterns, to cobbles, broken paving stones or just dirt tracks. A street may be right in the heart of things, action-packed with cars, people and colourful lights, or in a quiet area tucked away behind buildings or canals. Streets and roads all vary in size, length, usage, amount of traffic etc., and they can be private or public. A city street may carve its way through a jungle of skyscrapers, or wind gently through parkland.

Besides all the physical things that make up a streetscape, it changes according to the time of day, from the noisy clamour of the rush hour to the relaxed atmosphere of Friday nights. Some streets are inviting, friendly and warm, and some you avoid instinctively. Most people venture on to a street every day, even if it's only to get to the car or to grab lunch at midday. But how many really take notice of what is around them? It is so easy to miss things. You could walk down a street regularly for years, and then for some reason you might one day look up and notice a small statue high up on the roof of a building, or an alleyway you never saw before.

Even the common features of the street can provide amusement during routine journeys. There can't be many people who haven't played the game of watching for the cracks in the pavement and trying to avoid them, in case stepping on one of them sets off some terrible disaster. Near the end of my paper-round, I used to count every lamp-post or stair as I walked along, just to give more interest to the round and to make the time pass more quickly.

The streets are a part of the environment packed with all sorts of landmarks, excitements and dangers - which is why they have a whole chapter to themselves. There are endless things to be found on and around a street - bus stops, road signs, shops, street nameplates, trees, rubbish, white lines, lights, fences, tin cans, shadows, lumpy bits, smooth bits, level areas, hilly climbs, drainhole covers, paper blowing about, not to mention hazards such as dogs' droppings.

Normally, people move along a street in one way on the trip to school or work, and return later in the opposite direction to get home.

But to make an adventure of it you could move along it in any way: walking backwards, hopping between the paving stones, or walking only on the patches where the sun is shining.

Some activities may be unremarkable in a private area of a house or playground, but on the street, in public, they become a new sensation or a dare. Some silly games, like dressing up or acting stupidly, involve showing off or trying to keep a straight face. This can be a lot of fun in itself, without interfering with or upsetting the public; people may even enjoy watching it. A drama group may be great fun in a room with a few friends watching, but what about transferring it to the street with a real audience? The police will not bother you as long as you do not create a nuisance.

Some games can be used to get players to look at their local streets with a fresh eye, especially if the city is old. Street names often reflect the history of an area, or a past event. Some young people spend most of their childhood on the streets, so why not use this rather than turning a blind eye to the attractions.? You can introduce all sorts of sports to the city streets. Orienteering might sound dull, but given a more interesting name and a set of silly tasks to perform and things to collect on the way, it can be made more exciting and inviting. Taking photography out of the classroom and on to the streets becomes a great challenge, and makes you want to rush back to the darkroom to develop the film. Perhaps with a fun introduction to a new activity, the kids will develop an interest and want to continue with the activity themselves.

Many activities definitely take on a 'buzz' out on the streets among the public. The streets are full of dangers, and there is the risk of a player becoming so involved in a game that they forget the traffic or other hazards. I don't think the answer is to avoid these activities. It's up to the group to organise the game rules so that players are aware of the risks, and to reduce the dangers so that the game also becomes a road safety learning experience. Some games are simply not suitable for the streets at all. Some can be adapted by having a penalty included to prevent carelessness. An example might be the game of going along the street walking only on the sunny bits; the rule should be that all crossings have to be made at the lights or at a pedestrian crossing. Players would have to double back to avoid getting a penalty for a careless crossing in a dangerous part of the road where the sun was shining. Games all vary when played in different areas, so it's up to the leader and the group to set the safety ground rules for their own area, and it's everyone's responsibility to keep an eye out for forgetful players.

What about the law? As long as the game is not disturbing property, making a mess, misusing the surroundings or disturbing the peace, it should be all right. If in doubt, ask the police beforehand. Some games may need a note from the club to be carried in case the police stop players to ask what is going on. Games which involve lots of players at unusual times of day should perhaps be checked out with the police first. This is just so that they can advise you, or simply to let them know what's hit their patch for the day.

Not all street games have to be action-packed, outrageously daring or totally silly. You could go for a stroll – drive or walk downtown and simply amble along looking at the window displays and enjoying the odd sights and things that are going on. At the end of the stroll you might come across a tea stand, and after a cuppa you could drive to the club or back home just in time for bed. Or you could find a café with tables outdoors, and simply relax with a small group of friends.

Roads and streets are the biggest part of most cities, so use them both for fun and in an educational way, making the most of all the potential learning experiences.

THE GAMES

STREET HISTORY

In the older parts of large cities most of the streets, parks and buildings are named after something that happened or someone who lived in the past. The history of a street might have some connection with an old battle there, or with a famous person who worked in the area. It may even have something to do with the physical nature of the area, such as a nearby river that disappears underground. There are many of these rivers in London that people do not know are underneath them. Whatever a street's background, its history is normally very interesting. Local libraries will usually be of great help in finding out the details.

PAVEMENT NUDGE

This can be played along the street when you are on the way to somewhere. It can be played by two or more players, depending on how wide the pavement is. First, try it in pairs with someone the same size as you. Put your arms round each other as you stand side by side, then start to walk along the street treading only on smooth bits of pavements and not on any cracks or joins. The idea is to try to knock your partner on to the joins or a cracked piece of pavement, but only by nudging them with your hips. Each time you do stand on a crack you lose a life. After nine lives you lose the game, get a new partner and start again. You can try this with more than two players, or even form a chain. If you have one big player and two smaller ones, the big one can go in the middle and the two smaller ones have to gang up on the big one.

PAVEMENT GAPS AND CRACK DODGING

You probably remember trying to get along the street without standing on a cracked piece of pavement or a gap in between slabs. Well, in this game you need to set a target a mile or so away which you have to get to without touching any cracks. If you do, you have to go backwards for fifty paving stones. Try it with a partner, three-legged style. Two people could even do it while holding a large object between them, such as a short ladder with one person at each end. Sheer madness!!

A TO Z TREASURE HUNT

A to Z is the name given to books of maps that concentrate on the streets in different towns and cities; it maps them all out in nice, neat squares with every street named. A to Zs come in all different sizes and scales; you can even get them in colour. The idea of this game is for small groups to follow clues given by the leader using the A to Z. There may be twenty things they have to see or collect in a given area. (The area may simply be a double page in the map book, so that it is fairly easy to find the roads.) For example, a question might be what the graffiti says on the wall on the corner of Falmouth Road and Great Dover Street, or what is on at the cinema in Upper Street. This obviously does take a lot of work by the leader beforehand. Each group needs an A to Z, and players must stay together in their groups at all times. The groups are given the task and have half an hour to sit down and plan out their routes - each group can plan their own as they do not have to find the answers in any particular order. They all have to get back by a given time. When they meet, you count up how many answers or objects each group has found and how quickly they have done it. Each group needs one responsible member in it, and younger players need their parents' permission. If you have two groups, each could spend one week planning a task for the other to do the following week. A group is disqualified if they are not all together both during the game and at the end. The leaders will be driving around the streets in their cars to keep an eye on things.

ANAGRAM ROUTE FINDING

In this game you use the street nameplates that you find on the corners of buildings. You have to find a route by following street names on a pre-drawn-up list of which each team has been given a copy. The names are followed in order until you get to the last street, where someone will be waiting if you've followed the list correctly. Divide the group into small teams and set them off at five-minute intervals. All teams have to follow the same route. The catch is that each street name on the list has all its letters rearranged, so the players have to work out the real name. It's best done in an area the group is not familiar with, in case they work out the later street names and take short cuts. If one team catches up with another and decides to follow them, they may both find themselves going up the wrong street. The route needs to be worked out a few days beforehand from a map and then walked round by the organisers to check that the streets do still exist and the route works. Have a set time for all groups to meet in case some get lost - but not too near the last street as that will give them a clue as to the direction to take.

DRAMA WALKABOUT

Some clubs have drama groups, but often they spend their time stuck in a room away from everyone, except when they put on a show now and then or invite a few members in to watch. Well, how about moving out on to the street to act, or on to a tube train? You may have to get permission for this, and you must be careful not to disturb the peace or offend the public, but what a live experience! It could be a confidence-builder or a crusher, but the feelings, emotions and even embarrassment must all be good, healthy experiences for actors.

CITY WALK

In this activity you need to plan a route which can be anything from five miles to twenty-five miles. Work out the route so that it passes through many interesting areas, from fairgrounds to historic places, from quiet back streets to crowded market places. It can be just for fun, or run as a sponsored event to raise money for your club or a charity. The walk could either start and finish at your base or start from base and finish at a distant point, with a minibus waiting to bring back the walkers. People should stay in groups: no one should ever be left alone. Have a phone number anyone can ring if in trouble, and a spare mini-bus to pick up those who get too tired.

£10,000 WINDOW SHOPPING

This game involves a visit to an up-market part of town with a pen and a sheet of paper with £10,000 written on the top of the page. The aim is for everyone to wander around the shops and pretend to spend that amount of money. Every time you see something you really like, deduct the price from your account. You have to spend exactly the whole amount, not a penny more or less. At a given time you all meet up, go back to base and compare notes on what you spent and what you got for it. After the game, depression might well set in when you think of all the things you haven't got!

PICTURE TRAIL

This game might take a few weeks to prepare unless you have an instant camera. Divide the group into teams of about four people. Each team has a camera, or if there aren't enough they can take it in turns to use a camera at different times. Each team has to make a secret map using photos. Have a starting point and a destination, and walk the course with the camera. As you go along the street, take the odd photo of the area so that with a little looking around the others can recognise where the photo was taken. The idea is to build up a whole series of photos to direct another team to the destination. For example, when you come to a junction you will have to pick something obvious like a post-box down the street you want to go down (as long as there isn't another post-box in the other direction). Get each team to make up a map one week for another team to follow the next week. This game can be made easy or difficult, depending on the level of the group.

A variation of this is to divide the group into small teams, each team with an 'instant' camera. The teams walk around their local area, taking photos of *parts* of objects or buildings. The aim is to make it hard for other teams to guess the subject of the photo. Each person can take three pictures and after an hour the teams meet back at the club, to guess the subjects of the others' photos.

JOGGING

This is an activity that lots of people are getting into more and more. It's good fitness training, and can be done by a wide range of ages. You don't have to jog for miles, or be super-fit. First try jogging around the block, and then aim for a little further each time. Some people will hate the idea of jogging at first, but with the right encouragement they may give it a go and like it. Others will be willing to try it in a group, but not by themselves.

CAR NUMBER PLATES

There are quite a few games that people play while driving along as a passenger in a car and looking at other cars' number plates. This game is based on one of these, but it starts out from the club on foot with a pen and a notebook.

Divide into groups of four and make up a route for the groups to follow, arranging it so that they go in a big circle around the club. Each group of four is a team and can only return together as a team. The idea is for all teams to be let loose at the same time along the given route and look only at parked cars' number plates. Each person has to spell their first and last names from the letters on the plates. The letters can only be used in the right order, so if somebody's name is Jill then she cannot start until she sees a car with a J in it; if she sees an L first, that's not allowed. You can only go forwards not backwards. If you go all the way around the circuit and still have letters to get, then you may go round again. The four team members have to stick together until all their names are complete, then they must rush back to the club. The first team back wins. No shortened names are allowed, and if a plate has two letters of your name in the right order, you can use them both. If you have a letter in your name that is not used in car number plates, like I, then you are allowed to ignore it.

STREET SIGHTINGS

This is based on the idea that you could live in a particular area and regularly walk up and down the same street without really noticing what is around you. Divide the players into groups of three or four, and give each group a photocopy of a map of the area you want to cover, which should be an area of about one square mile. Each group has the same area. The groups have to go out and walk around these streets and parks with a pen and notebook and jot down anything of interest that they have not noticed before, like the statue above the fire station wall, or what is actually says under the monument in the main street. After a given time they all meet back at the base and compare notes on what they have seen. You could easily turn this into a quiz or some sort of competition.

BLIND NOSE TRAIL

The group is divided up into pairs and driven to an unfamiliar area. One member of each pair is blindfolded for the whole journey. When they arrive, the sighted members help their blindfolded partners out of the vehicle and take them for a walk. To guide a blindfolded person, let them hold your elbow and walk one step behind you, not in front. Each pair has a fifteen-minute walk. The idea is that the blindfolded person must identify some of the noises they hear as they go along, and at the end of the walk their partner tells them whether they were right or wrong. You may walk past a train station, docklands or market place, for example, so there should be lots of noises, both obvious and subtle, going on. The sighted person is not allowed to speak until the end of the walk. When you have finished, change places and do it again. It is a good idea to have a practice run at guiding beforehand.

PHOTO ME AND THE OBJECT

There are two ways to play this game, but basically you get a photo taken of you with an object. One way of playing is to show very clearly what the object is; it could be you next to a lamp-post or statue, or inside a telephone box. The other way is to take a series of photos of you and the object which don't make it very obvious what it is. The object could be a coke can, a letter-box or a hat which is on someone's head in one photo and in a dustbin in another. You can work in pairs, taking photos of each other. Get all the different pairs together one evening and let them present their photos one at a time, seeing if the others can guess what the object is.

TAPE SOUND TRAILS

For this game you need two simple tape recorders. Divide the group into two teams, each having one of the tape recorders. In the morning the teams go their separate ways with a tape recorder and a secret prize treasure that is to be hidden at the end of the trail. As you leave the base you have to speak the directions you are travelling on to the tape. For example: turn left, walk past the phone box, pass the pond, have a cup of tea in Pete's café, get on the Underground from the Angel to King's Cross, walk up to platform four, get a platform ticket; at the end of the platform, behind a fire bucket, is the prize. Both groups meet back at the base for lunch, and not a word is spoken about the route. In the afternoon the teams swap tapes and can only play it once as they try to follow it to find the hidden treasure. Don't play the whole tape in one go! Play the first instruction, and follow it, then play the next, and so on. You can go anywhere and make it as easy or as hard as you think best for the group. The main thing is to make it as interesting and as mad as possible. The trail can be as long as the tape lasts. I think an hour's journey is about right.

SOUNDS OF THE CITY

For this game you again need a tape recorder; if you have more than one, that is better still. The idea is that you go out on to the streets and take some recordings, then bring them back and see if people can recognise them. If you have lots of teams with a tape recorder each, you can use the recordings in the form of a quiz, or a very difficult treasure trail with just street sounds as a guide, no proper instructions. If you pick the right noises, it just might work. But simply trying to work out what the noises are could be fun enough.

CARE FOR THE EGG

This activity can have a sticky end if you're not careful. Each player is given a real egg which they have to look after and guard with their life. If the egg breaks, they are out of the game and will probably miss out on an omelette later. The activity can be a short one – for example the egg is a small bomb and you have to transport it over an obstacle course – or it can be an all-day adventure beginning in the morning with the theme that the egg is a baby and you have to look after it for the whole day. The egg has to be carried all day through thick and thin: if you have a shower, then the egg has to have one too; if you are canoeing or rock climbing, it has to go along as well. It's up to you to protect and care for it. Get together at the end of the day and see if everyone still has the egg they started with – or tell the sad story! Do you think you could manage to take an egg around with you for a whole day at school or at work?

DINING OUT

In this book there are some activities where you make meals at the club. Well, this one is to get paired up with another member and take each other out for a meal. Each player has to put £2.50 into a kitty so that when pairs are picked, they are given five pounds to live it up with. The idea is to go out for any sort of meal you fancy without spending more than five pounds. Make a note of where you went, how you spent the evening and what things cost. At the next club night each pairs goes through their list. You will have to decide how to pick pairs. It might be out of a hat, one of each sex, people choosing a partner they may wish to meet and get to know better, or whatever you think best for the group. If your group is older, you will have to allow them more money (unless they go up the chippie!).

SILENT WALKING

This is a game I used to play when I was younger, but I had forgotten about it until I was in Mexico and saw a couple of boys playing it. The idea is to walk along without making any noise at all, so that means you have to move softly as you walk and be very careful about where you put your feet: they must not land on drainhole covers in case they creak, or on a stone that may rub along the pavement. You have to keep your wits about you all the time, especially if there's any sand about on the street.

When I saw this game being played again, I walked back to my hotel in the dark trying it out, and I thought I was doing well until I bumped into a couple with my head down looking straight at the ground. All three of us jumped a mile. Their English was non-existent, so I just said sorry and got out of sight quickly. You *can* do it at night as well as during the day, but mind other people!

PAPER TRAIL

In this game two people have to go off and hide, then after five minutes the rest of the group have to find them. The first two carry lots of paper and have to leave a trail for the others to follow. This trail can be as subtle or as obvious as you like, depending on who is playing. The hunters have to pick up the paper as they go along, for various reasons: firstly, the runners are still on the move and could double back; secondly, the next two runners will need paper to use; and thirdly, you don't want to leave any litter. One of the leaders should have a whistle in case they have to stop the game and call all the players back to the start, for example when the game has gone on too long, or a wind has picked up and blown the clues away. The paper clues can have rocks on top of them or be attached to twigs to stop them blowing away, but you must be able to see them. You could have a time limit on each game. You must leave a piece of paper at least every hundred yards, and every time you turn a corner or take a new direction.

SKIP HUNTING

The next time your club needs some furniture or wood, you could go skip hunting. A skip is one of those big metal things plonked on the road in everyone's way with no lights on at night and overflowing with rubbish for weeks. If you have a look around you can find almost anything in a skip. Do not dig down into them or open up bags. Simply rescue the odd table or chair from the top.

SKIPOLOGY

This is simply the study of the types of stuff people throw out into skips. You all go out and write down the sorts of things you come across in skips, as well as what areas the various skips were in. You could visit different areas to carry out your skipology project. You don't need to pull all the rubbish out, or tunnel down; just look, and write down what is obvious. The sorts of things you may find are lampshades, doors, old vacuum cleaners, rusty bikes, armchairs etc.

WATER GAMES

People often think there is very little water to use in cities, and are sometimes surprised to come across a river in the middle of one. In fact, many towns and cities were founded on the banks of a river, and then expanded in every direction. Water takes many forms, from rivers, canals, streams, flood-relief channels, reservoirs, lakes, ponds, gravel pits, fountains, indoor and outdoors swimming pools and paddling pools, to everyday rain and puddles. Not all of these are open to the public, or even safe, and each type has its own characteristics. Some reservoirs are open for general uses such as walking, fishing and water sports. You will have to look into the permits and regulations in your area, as they vary from place to place. You must also make sure you have suitable people with life-saving skills in attendance.

In this chapter I concentrate mainly on activities in swimming pools, as there is plenty written elsewhere on outdoor waterways. Swimming pools have really changed over the last five years in a lot of areas. You may remember the old red-brick building containing a square pool, with the paint coming off the walls and a few bugs running round your feet. During the day one or two old men might swim up and down, dodging in and out of the school group. A few children might come in to mess around and get thrown out for splashing, and after 6 p.m. you would often see the swimming or sub-aqua club. The new pool caters for a much wider community. Some pools have completely new buildings, while others still have the outside shell of the old building but with a clean and modern interior. Many new pools have introduced activities other than straightforward swimming. The family pools aim for a mixed layout, with shelved shallow areas for smaller children, nervous adults and the disabled. Wave machines and water slides have been introduced for the more adventurous. There is increased use of pools by adults, both in the evenings and at lunch-time. In fact, there are so many different types of groups using the pools today that it's often hard to find a time-slot for a group session. However, the whole pool can usually be hired, either for one-off events or on a regular basis. You need to chat with your local pool manager about insurance and safety regulations, as these vary from area to area.

Some of the pool-based activities you can find now are swimming, diving, canoeing, sub-aqua, snorkelling for younger groups, life-saving, polo, water exercises, keep fit, water splash and fun activities, adult beginners' swimming lessons, parent and toddlers clubs and therapeutic work, and some places even hire out the pool for opera singers or musical groups to record in.

An active pool will have various bits of equipment, such as floating mats, canoes, snorkelling gear, and ramps and chairs for lifting people with particular disabilities. Any activity, unless it is progressive, can become dull after a few months, so a few games and activities help to keep interest alive.

Snorkelling can be great fun, but after a lot of training there is a chance of it becoming stale. Liven it up by getting permission to sink some objects, such as chairs, to swim through. Or sink a cupboard and use plastic air-bags to 'salvage' it. These activities still teach skills, but are a lot more enjoyable than routine practice.

It's very important to have a good working relationship with the pool manager, so that you can discuss your activities beforehand. Some clubs divide the pool into different areas and have various activities going on at the same time. Remember that whatever the activity, a trained watchful eye at the pool-side is a must, and a lot of common sense is needed. Water can be dangerous. The fun must never outweigh people's safety.

The nice thing about an indoor swimming pool is that it is a comfortable, protected environment all year round, and if you're lucky the water is generally warm. More or less anyone – young or old, able-bodied or disabled – can get involved in pool activities, as most of these can be adapted to suit the people involved. For example, we were once having some silly races where you had to blow a ping-pong ball from one end of the pool to the other, keeping it afloat without touching it. By the pool there was a young lad who could not use his arms and legs, and we invited him to play. (He spoke only Icelandic, which was a bit of a problem!) In the end we simply adapted the game a little by playing across the width at the shallow end with one person supporting him. It was a close race!

Some people can control the underwater lights, which is fun. If there are specator seats around the pool you could put on a display such as a canoe ballet or a pantomime with sub-aqua divers. Even the most serious and competitive swimming clubs have some fun at the end of a hard session, which helps to push and stimulate their muscles to do that little bit more work.

THE GAMES

LOG ROLLING

If there is some water near your club, try to get hold of a large section of a fallen tree, or an old telegraph pole. Simply place it on the water and try to stand upright on it. When you can do that, try to run on it like a real logger. Don't forget a change of clothes!

SNORKELLING RELAY RACES

There are endless ways of organising snorkelling relays in the pool. It is a good method of keeping fit and learning to fin some distance. One idea is for each team to sink all its snorkelling equipment at one end of the pool. On the word 'GO' one member of each team has to swim up from the other end, fit their equipment on and then fin back; then the next person can go. The first team to finish wins - as long as they have their own gear on.

SNATCH SNORKEL

Divide the players into two teams which go to opposite ends of the swimming pool. Everyone wears full snorkelling gear, but with the snorkel inverted so that the mouthpiece is at the top. The two teams face one another, each player having an opposing contestant to battle with. The idea is to snatch the other person's snorkel without getting your own snatched. You are allowed to touch only the snorkel, no other piece of equipment nor the opponent's body. When a snorkel has been snatched, the player who still has their snorkel has to get to the other end of the pool without losing it. You cannot take a snorkel once your opponent has reached the other end. If the game goes on too long with a couple repeatedly catching each other, have a three-minute countdown to finish. The team with the most snorkels win. Snorkels must not be used to breathe through during this game. You may decide to snatch only the fins in the next game.

MARCO POLO

This is a game played in a swimming pool with a group of about ten players or more. Pick one player who has to keep their eyes closed all the time; the others keep their eyes open. All the players have to stay in the water throughout the game. The idea is that 'MARCO', the blind player, has to catch the others, who are called 'POLO'. Marco walks around with arms outstretched, trying to grab someone. At any time they want, the blind player can call out 'Marco' and the others must immediately shout back 'Polo'. This gives Marco a chance to catch someone. When a person is caught then they become Marco, and the old Marco becomes a Polo. The only problem I can foresee is that there may be other people in the pool who are not playing, and they might not take too kindly to being grabbed!

MAT BALL POLO

Some swimming pools nowadays have large foam mats for people to play on. If you are lucky enough to be close to a pool where there are a lot of mats, you could have one each to sit or stand on as it floats around the pool. Divide the group into two teams and play a game where you have to keep passing the ball to your own team members and try to hit some sort of goal. Each end has a goal. You can move around the pool on the mats, but not with the ball - you have to pass it straight away. If you are passing the ball to a team member and it falls into the water, you have to give it to the nearest member of the other team. Change ends when one team has got five goals, and the winner is the first to ten.

FIN POLO

This is played like water polo, but all the players wear fins. No snorkels and masks are allowed. You play with a light football and score by hitting goals which can be a net or a board about 2 feet square, at the opposite end of the pool. You may catch the ball with two hands, but you can only throw it with one. There is no physical contact, and travelling with the ball is not permitted. After every goal, each team returns to its own end and the ball is thrown into the middle. Set a time limit, and change ends half-way through.

ANT RAFT

Ant raft was inspired by a film about ants working together to make bridges over gaps by linking up and acting as a team. It is played on a canal or river. A group of about ten or more is on the bank with canoes and paddles, ready to start. One by one the canoes are put on the water side by side, and members of the group get on to the forming raft and lie across the decks. When all the canoes are on the water, the group should be equally spread over the tops of the canoes, holding it together. The following are two ideas you can try.

1. Build an ant raft to paddle or use the wind to cross the canal or river.
2. Build an ant bridge to cross a small stream. The bridge starts by one bank and ends at the other. A few extra people can try to walk across the ant bridge from one bank to the other.

WATER SNAKE

This is another canoe game, and the idea is to tie all the boats together with small individual pieces of rope to form one long chain or 'snake'. The game can be played with as few as two people or as many as have canoes, and you can either spread out a few players along the chain or fill each boat. Both single and double canoes can form a part of the chain. This game may be useful for a club if it opens up for the day and only a few people drift in. You could keep it simple by just paddling around near the club, or you could go on a small journey which includes an easy portage or some tight turns, then return backwards. Keep an eye out for capsizes in the middle of the chain when doing tight turns quickly.

UNDERWATER FOOTBALL

The is a simple game of football with one major difference: the pitch is a swimming pool. The ideal depth is about 4 to 5 feet. You use a normal football, preferably an old one as you make a small hole in it just big enough to insert some lead weights and let in water so that it sinks to the bottom. The game is played in the same way as football, by using the feet to kick and with a goal at each end. One of the pretty coloured balls will do nicely. Some parks have shallow paddling pools of about 1 foot in depth, and you could use these with either a floating or a sinking ball. The water resistance will provide a lot of fun in the deep pool, whereas the paddling-pool game will have lots of spray and splashing.

SALVAGE PROJECT

This game is great fun in the swimming pool, but make sure you get permission from the manager. The idea is to sink a large object to the bottom of the pool at the deep end and then try to salvage it. This may simply be a chair, or a much larger object such as a metal locker. (One club I know of made a large fibreglass cannon to salvage.) Wearing full snorkelling gear, you need to try to lift the object to the surface using plastic carrier bags or proper lifting air-bags. First you attach the bags with string around the object, and then start filling them with air by holding your breath and blowing into them. Put a bit of air into a different bag each time, so that the object rises slowly and evenly. The closer the bags are to the object, the closer to the surface it will come. Remember, whatever you sink, it must be clean!

LONG-DISTANCE FLYING COMPETITION

Even though the aeroplane can now travel at twice the speed of sound, we still have a primitive need to try to fly under our own steam. You need a good location for this activity, which could be over either water or land. If it is over land you could use a sandpit or some foam to land on. The idea is to make your own wings or simple flying machine. You could use bed sheets, cloth, cardboard, old sails, sticks, broom handles, string and tape. If you wanted to get mechanical, you could use pram wheels and push-bikes to build up speed. If you are flying over water, make sure you can get free from your rig without any trouble. Remember to remove any rubbish you drop in the water. You could plan this event for the same day, or a week later so you can spend more time making the rig. You need a run-up to a ramp to take off. Have a rescue team ready.

If you want to judge the entries, the following might help.

1 Artistic Interpretation
Wing or rig design
Take-off and flight style
Splash-down technique, or landing if on land

2 Distance flown from take-off to splash-down or landing

The judge's decision is final.

WATER SKIM SURF

This game is played on water and uses a sheet of old wood that can just about float by itself. The wood should be about 4 feet by 8 feet and about an inch thick. First place the wood on the water a few feet out from the edge. Then walk back a few yards, take a run-up and jump on to the board. It will then skim across the surface while you are in a surfing position. As the board starts to slow down, it also starts to sink with you on it. You can control it a little bit by moving forwards or backwards, but eventually it will go down and you will get wet unless you can jump on to land. If there are pontoons or the banks are close to each other, you can try to skim surf from one side to another. If you get good at it and are still dry, why not double up with a friend and try it together?

DOG AND BONE

The group wears full snorkelling gear, and divides into two equal teams which go to opposite ends of the pool. Each person is given a number – the same numbers for both teams, but with no one knowing who has the corresponding number to theirs in the other side. An object that will sink is thrown into the middle of the pool by the instructor, and a number is called. The person from each team with that number has to do a step entrance and fin as quickly as possible to see who can get to the object first. They then return to their teams and a new number is called.

POOL SUMP DIVING

This comes from a dangerous manoeuvre in caving where the caver has to go underwater and come up again the other side into air. The activity can be used as a game in the swimming pool, as part of a snorkelling club session, or as serious training practice for cavers. In any event, it needs constant supervision. A simple try at it would be to sink a couple of chairs in the pool and swim through them to get the feel of it; then you can add more chairs to make an underwater tunnel with a rope going through it, with the players wearing blacked-out masks so they can only feel the rope and not see it. If you get on well with the pool manager, you might be able to turn the lights off and use torches underwater, but the pool *must* be adequately supervised. You may be able to use a short tube of the type they now use on building sites to dump rubbish down. But whatever you use, make sure that if someone gets out of breath they can push the tunnel apart or away so they can swim to the surface for air. Diving clubs may try it with air tanks. The instructor in charge must set the safety guidelines.

CANOE HORSEBACK ROLL

For canoeists, this is a good test of balance and timing. You need to put a spray deck on the boat without you in it - this keeps the water out as you tie up the trunk. Turn the canoe upside down and sit on it as if you are on horseback, with a leg either side. The aim is to roll the canoe all the way round without falling off or getting your body wet. You do it in stages, by turning the canoe on one edge, upside down on the other edge, then finishing in the upright position.

SKI DRAG

This idea came from being pulled uphill while on a skiing holiday, which was a nice experience. All you need are a length of rope and a few people to pull you along. You could be on roller skates, a go-kart or a skateboard. But the best version is on water, where you jump on a sheet of plywood of about 8 feet by 4 feet while holding one end of a rope with a stick tied to it; a few friends hold the other end and run along the bank. You stand on the wood near the back, and it should hold your weight as it comes up on the plane. When you feel at home, you can try some tricks like backward riding and 360° turns.

MAT RACING

Many swimming pools now have fun hours when they bring out floating toys and mats for people to play on. If you have a large group of about twenty or more people and there are enough mats, split up the players into equal teams so that each team has a mat. Line up the mats at one end of the pool, and get the players to lie on them face down with their knees and feet in the water. If they all wear fins, that will be even better. On the word 'GO' they have to kick or fin as fast as possible to the other end. Arms and hands can only be used for holding on to the mat. The first team to the opposite end wins.

POOL BOAT

If your club or local swimming pool has a small plastic rowing boat, you could use it in your snorkelling class to practise pool entries and exits with your gear on. Make sure you ask for permission, and that the boat is clean. The activity can be a teaching aid or just a fun event. You could even use it in a display.

OCTOPUSH

This is an underwater game of hockey for snorkellers and divers, and there are international rules that the game can be played by. A simplified version would be to have two teams wearing full gear, and a hand-held pusher which is a bit of wood about 8 inches long, shaped like a letter 'T'. You need a heavy puck about 4 inches wide that will sink. The players take a deep breath at the surface, dive down to push the puck towards the goal, and then come back up for more air to carry on. Each team has a goal at the opposite end of the pool. For the proper rules and details, contact the National Snorkellers Club.

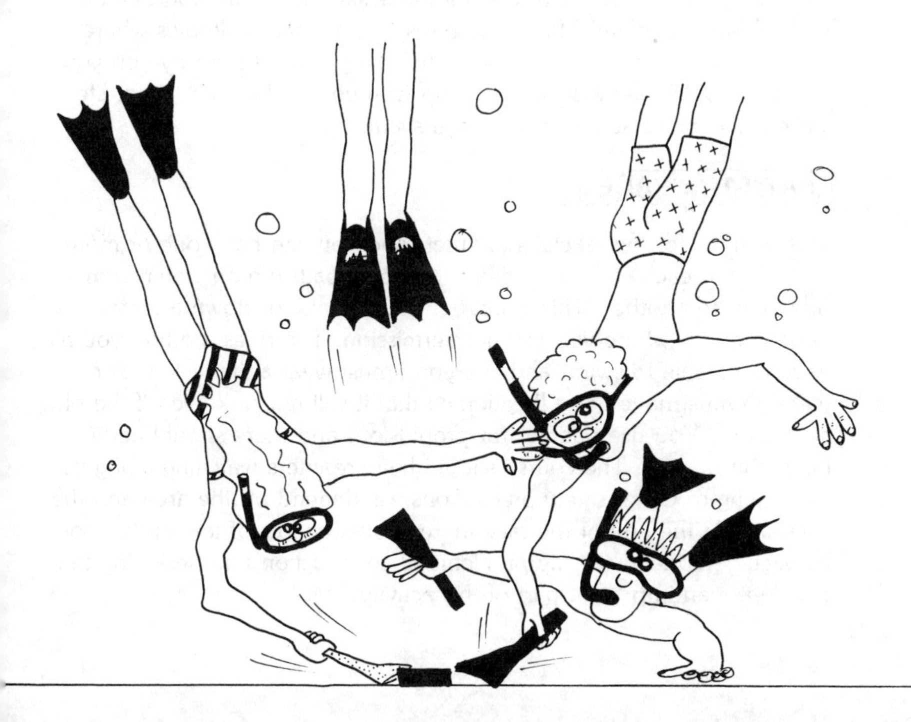

SHARKS AND DOLPHINS

This game uses snorkelling gear in the swimming pool. Two players are the 'sharks' and they wear blacked-out masks so they cannot see. (Use waterproof parcel tape to black out the masks). The rest of the group are 'dolphins'. The sharks swim all around the pool while the dolphins try to swim as close to them as possible without being grabbed. When a dolphin has been caught it then swims to the side and waits for the next game. When two sharks meet they shout out 'SHARK' and swim off in different directions. After a set time of, say, five minutes you stop the game and get two new sharks. If the sharks catch every dolphin, then they win; if not, then the dolphins win. If a person who is supposed to be a dolphin goes nowhere near the sharks, they are a 'slug'.

LAKE SAILBOAT CAMP

If there is a local pond, lake, reservoir or somewhere you can go sailing, and you feel like a bit of a change with a touch of adventure, why not plan a night camp on a dinghy. Take a few bits of bedding, some polythene to make a roof if it looks like rain, some food and a flask of hot chocolate. Make sure a responsible person knows where you are and what you are doing so that they can keep an eye on you, or have a older member of the group with you in the boat. Wear life-jackets and make sure everyone can swim.

BATH-TUB RACE

This event is for lots of clubs to enter, and you can have one or more entries from each club. The idea is to race a bath-tub on water from one point to another. This could be across a lake or down a river, depending on where you can get permission. The rules are that you all have to be able to swim, and everyone must wear a life-jacket. The bath-tub must have good flotation so that it will not sink even if the plug comes out. You use paddles for propulsion, and there should be two people in the tub. The course should have rescuers watching along its entire length. Other safety precautions will depend on the area and the weather. At the end of the race there should be lots of tea and a good barbecue. Working out the problems of construction and designing the course are an important part of this activity.

DEAF ALPHABET

Some deaf people use their hands to communicate. There is a finger sign for each letter of the alphabet. Some people think this is just for hearing-impaired people, but that's not true as hearing people need it so that they can communicate with the deaf. There are lots of ways to use these signs for fun, particularly when other types of communication aren't any good. For example, you could use them underwater when snorkelling or diving, in strong winds, or even behind glass. Invent your own activities after a short lesson to learn the signs. You may even want to go and learn more about signing and other forms of communication, and maybe invite some deaf people to come and try the underwater activities. Local or national organisations for the deaf can supply you with cards to help you learn the correct signs.

WET VOLLEYBALL

Volleyball is a fun game that all sorts of people can enjoy together. Some players can really let themselves go, whereas others who, like me, are getting a little bit older and more delicate, worry about falling and hitting the floor. To avoid the bumps, you could play it in a swimming pool that has a fairly level bottom. Just stretch a net across the pool, and find a ball.

CARDBOARD BOATS

The idea in this task is to build your own boat of some sort and to cross a section of water in it. The boat can take any form, from a canoe to a raft. You could even have a team effort and make a Viking-type boat or a battleship. The main point is that is must be made only from cardboard, and no other materials. The only things that can be used to help are some form of joining tape, staples and string. Any sails, rudders or rigging have to be cardboard. The water you want to cross can be a pond, river, stream or canal. Water *is* dangerous, so make sure everyone can swim. Wear life-jackets and have a lifeguard on duty. If it is a large section of water, a proper rescue boat is needed. The activity can be an individual event, or part of a larger occasion. You could also have side events going on, like a cardboard camera filming the boat crossing, with commentary.

FIGURE-OF-EIGHT SAILING

Racing sail crafts is a useful skill, and can be good fun. There are lots of different courses to race around. Try sailing in a figure-of-eight formation, with two boats. This can be very exciting, as you have to cross each other's path in the middle of the course. The idea is to try to be first back to your starting point, miss each other on the way, and just enjoy it.

CANOE MATCHSTICK RACE

This game can be played in a swimming pool or on a river, canal or lake. Each player sits in a canoe on the water, and all the paddles are taken from them and placed in an area of water like lots of matchsticks floating around. On the word 'GO' the players have to use their hands to get to the paddles and find their own, then race back to the starting point. The more players the better.

BRANCH RAFT

There are all sorts of things you can use to make rafts, from cardboard boxes, canoes and old oil drums to almost anything that floats. Here we try a more traditional design used in the Caribbean; the raft is made out of bamboo canes all lashed together side by side. I doubt very much whether you have a lot of bamboo lying around where you live, but you can use branches from a local park after they have been cutting and trimming the trees. You need lengths of about 12 to 15 feet long and about 4 inches thick. You'll probably have to improvise a bit. Lash the branches together until the raft is about 6 feet wide with a few cross-pieces. You can have some low seats if you want. You propel the raft along with a pole or thinner branch. Wood doesn't float very well, so your feet are going to get wet. A well-built raft can shoot some small rapids, but it is not a seaworthy craft in this state so it is for inshore calm water and you should wear safety life-jackets. Maybe you could go over the top and have some melons, mangoes and bananas on board, followed by a fruit drink to wash it all down.

POOL PARTNERS CATCH-BALL

This pool game is best with groups of about twelve or more, and all you need are a swimming pool and a football. Divide the group into pairs. One person in each pair gets into the water and the other is left walking around the edge. Everyone spreads out and the ball is thrown into the pool. The players in the pool have to try to grab the ball and throw it out to their partner. A goal is scored when a pool player gets it to their partner. If a player picks up the ball on the side but it wasn't thrown by their partner, it is not a goal - but they can throw it to their partner in the water so that they can throw it back. The first pair to ten wins, the partners all swap places, and a new game starts. Depending on the group, you will have to decide whether or not the players may grab each other. If the pool floor is slippery, you will have to ban any running.

SPLASH DAY

A splash day is normally held during school holidays at a local public swimming pool. Anything goes - except straightforward swimming. There are various events held throughout the day. There may be rope swings, large foam mats to play on, lots of buckets with a good supply of sponges to throw at each other, and many other events. The pool is always watched by trained lifeguards and there is an overall organiser to run the show and not let it get out of hand.

YANK THEM IN

This is a type of tug-of-war over water (e.g. a swimming pool or large puddle), with only one person at each end of the rope. The idea is to try to pull the other person into the water. Both stand by the edge holding the rope, then pull or jerk the rope trying to catch the other person off balance. You must not tie yourself to the rope, and players are only allowed to let go of the rope three times; after that, they have to throw themselves in. If it is too easy, then turn around and try it back to back, still with the water between you. Maybe we should call this one wash day!

POOL PUFFING RACE

This game is played in a swimming pool and can really get those lungs working hard. All the players line up side by side at the shallow end, each with an object to puff along. This object must float; you could use arm-bands, swim floats or even ping-pong balls. Ideally, they should all be the same size. On the command 'GO' everybody has to blow their object to the opposite end without physically touching it. The player whose object first touches the other end wall wins. If the other end is deep and there are small children playing, then the game can be played across the shallow end instead. Have at least one adult at the pool-side watching for safety, as you would with any game around water. Encourage the players not to puff too rapidly, as they may hyperventilate which could result in a blackout.

SAILING DODGEMS

The people who maintain these boats will go mad when they hear of this game, but they shouldn't. Play in a large set area of a local lake or pond which has lots of old or plastic sailing boats, each player in their own boat. The aim is to sail everywhere and anywhere, dodging in and out of every other player. Remember that the idea is to *dodge,* unlike fairground dodgems which often bump – fine for them, but it would certainly sink a sailing boat in the end. Your reflexes and turning skills will be pushed to the limit in this one. For swimmers only.

LARGE GROUPS

By large groups I mean anything from twenty to two hundred people involved in a game. With such large numbers of players, you obviously need a big area to play in. This could be an indoor hall, a playground, or an open space such as a park or woodland (unless you are trying to see how many people you can fit into the broom cupboard or telephone box!).

With so many people involved you need good communication and organisation, so that everyone knows what's what. When talking to the whole group, be clear when explaining instructions and rules – as soon as the game has started, it will be hard to stop. In large open areas, you should have boundaries; this will help keep the game under control and make it work. For instance, in *Hide and Seek,* if there are no boundaries, some players could well go home for lunch and return an hour later claiming first prize because no one has caught them.

It's a nice idea to invite a few local clubs along so you can compete with each other in club teams or have players mixed up within teams. If it's done well, getting together like this can help to break down a few prides and prejudices. Getting to know other club members may lead to new activities, sharing equipment and combining trips. When you get a large group of people together for the first time, many of them do not know each other, and a few fun activities may break the ice a little. You could have one big game, where the whole group is spilt into two teams; or you could try a lot of smaller events, where people move around a circuit of activities. An example could be a silly athletics meeting with wet sponges used as shot puts, or brooms still with their heads on as javelins.

Team-work is an important part of these group activities. Some people much prefer large team games to individual pursuits, and like to get 'lost' within a big group. These large group games are a good way to let off steam and energy. And it can be interesting to see the group dynamics within the teams. You soon get familiar roles emerging: the leaders, the jokers, the clumsy ones, the sporty types and the lazy drifters.

On the safety side, it's a good idea to have some sort of code that everyone knows beforehand, like a whistle for half-time where groups change roles, or, more importantly, a signal to bring everyone back in an emergency.

An activity doesn't have to be fantastically organised days beforehand. If it's a nice day you could simply go over to the park for the afternoon. But if it's a big, complicated game with lots of clubs involved, a printed information sheet with meeting times, venue and rules could be sent out in advance. Group leaders should watch carefully for members not getting involved, and perhaps help them to be more enthusiastic by giving them a role which holds their interest.

Another nice idea after a long day of activities is to have a couple of hours' break, then all meet up again for the evening and have a barbecue or disco. If it's been a night activity, then you should definitely meet for breakfast. This would be the best part for me, with a large bacon sandwich and a mug of tea!

THE GAMES

BRITISH BULLDOG

This game has been played for years all over the country and without too much variation. It is a very physical game with lots of contact. Here I want to explain the basics of the game and suggest how you could vary it. The game can be played inside or outside, preferably on soft grass or mats, and needs a square-shaped pitch with some sort of lines or walls at each end. One person is 'on' and has to catch the others as they run past. The other players all line up at one end, either behind a line or touching a wall. When the catcher shouts 'British Bulldog', all the players have to run to the line at the opposite end, trying to keep out of the way of the catcher. To catch a player you can either lift the player off the ground or lay them on the ground and shout 'one, two, three British Bulldog'. When you are caught you are on with the catcher, and the first one caught is on in the next game. Strong people can barge past the catcher and smaller, weaker players can dodge in and out to avoid being caught.

The game can be adapted to suit any group. You could mark out an area in the park with dozens of trees in the way. It could be played on the side of a hill where the players have to run up and down. The method of catching people could also vary. For example, everyone could wear hats which have to be taken off for a player to be caught. You could wear arm-bands that have to be removed, or carry water-filled balloons which the catcher has to burst to catch you. How about playing it in total darkness?

COWBOYS AND INDIANS

This game can be played around large estates or in a wooded part of the local park. You should wear old clothes (as you do for many of the activities in this book). Split the group into two teams, one being the cowboys and the other the indians. Everyone has a weapon – a large felt-tip pen, each of a different colour. The teams go off in different directions to find a base. After ten minutes a whistle is blown to start the war. The idea is for each team to go out and catch one of the other team and bring them back to their base as a prisoner. This is where the pens come in: they are used to 'brand' prisoners' faces with the team mark. After a given time the whistle will blow to end the game, and you count how many prisoners each team has caught. The one with the most wins the battle.

LUNATICS AND WARDENS

When I was young this was one of my favourite games; the name alone makes it sound exciting. It can be played inside or out, and you need about twelve to twenty players. Divide the group into two equal halves. One team are the lunatics and the others are the wardens. The game should have a time limit of about thirty minutes or more per team, unless all the lunatics are caught beforehand. A prison is made out of chairs or a rope around some trees. In the middle of the prison is a chair with a can or ball on it. There must be an opening to the prison, and players can only get in and out through this. The game can now start.

The lunatics run off and hide while the judge starts the time countdown. After two minutes the wardens have to go out and find the lunatics and bring them to the prison. This might mean carrying them as they try to get away, or you can decide that a touch will do if the players are young or rather timid. Once there are lunatics in the prison they must stay there until they are released by another team member not yet caught, who has to sneak up and rush into the prison via the opening and knock the object off the chair; the others are then free to run away again. When the time is up, count how many are in the prison, then call everybody together again and change roles. The winning team is the one with the most caught when the time is up. You will need to define a playing area that you have to stay within. This game is fun for players of any age. Lots of tactics can be used, and it's up to each team to decide how many players go out and catch and how many guard the prison.

TAG-ON

This is a very popular game with young people and is usually played outside, although it can be played inside if the building is very large with lots of hiding places. One person is 'on' to start with and has to close his/her eyes while the others hide within an agreed area. When the catcher has waited for a few minutes, they go out and try to find the others. When they do find and touch another player, that player is on with them; this goes on until every player has been found and touched. The game is fun during the day, but even better at night. The first one caught is on in the next game.

THE PIED PIPER

This activity can be played by as few as thirty youngsters or as many as four hundred, when it really comes alive. It can be an activity in itself, or part of a large festival. The young people are asked weeks beforehand to make themselves a costume to wear on the theme the Pied Piper, so they can choose to dress up as rats, little children or the Pied Piper himself. Get everyone to meet up in the park at a given time, and have an adult dressed as the Pied Piper and playing a pipe.

You will already have worked out a march route through town, with the help of the police. If there is a local community circus with lots of stilt-walkers and jugglers, get them to join in to add an extra bit of colour. The walk should be fun in itself, but when you end up back at base it would be nice to have some games organised, and perhaps a barbecue or refreshments of some sort.

STAFF V YOUNG PEOPLE

This is not a game but rather an idea that can be used with many of the games in this book. It could be anything from a simple game of football to a major commando hunt at night. Sometimes it's useful to let the young people have a chance to get their own back on members of staff, especially if there is water or mud involved! You could even devote the last two weeks of term to a staff against youngsters competition, with three or four events each evening. A large timetable of events is put up on the wall with people putting their names down for the activities they want to enter. You can have a mixture of activities, from normal sports to bizarre, silly events like doughnut eating or water-bomb throwing. It's a good way of bringing staff and young people closer together.

TREASURE HUNTS

A treasure hunt can be anything from an instant simple game with a few surprises hidden within a small area, to a grand event that takes days to plan, with complicated clues carefully placed over a wider area. Get together and think of how you can adapt a treasure hunt to suit the level of your group.

CLUB INFORMATION HUNT

You can run your own club hunt, where you have typed lists of questions and each individual has to run around the clubhouse finding the answers to them. All the questions are about the club itself, like how many steps there are in the building, how many doors, toilets, windows, paving stones, heaters, and so on. You have a set time to find out the information and then report back. The player who answers the most questions correctly wins. Can you imagine having to count all the floorboards in the grand hall?

PUNISHMENT RUN-OUTS

The game needs a lot of players divided into two equal teams. First, get everyone together and invent dozens of punishments you will give to players who get caught. They could be something like the following.

1 Sing a song
2 Do ten press-ups
3 Climb a tree, up to 10 feet high
4 Scream 'I love you' as loudly as possible
5 No talking for two minutes

One team runs out in a set area and the others follow in three minutes, all carrying a sheet of paper with the various punishments written on it. Secretly you give each punishment a number, so that when you catch one of the other team they choose a number and you then tell them what they have to do. If they do it they are set free, but if they refuse they are out of the game and you tell the others they are out. The game is played for thirty minutes each way. A signal is sounded or a flag raised at half-time to bring both groups back to the start to change roles.

HUNT THE LEADER

This game is for a large group of young people and adults. You need twenty to thirty adults and about sixty to eighty youngsters. All the young players need to know the adults fairly well. The adults are the leaders and have to disguise themselves and go into a given area of town. The area should be about half a square mile in size. A leader could dress up as a police officer, road sweeper or vicar, or even pretend to be an old lady praying inside a church. I've seen some really funny ideas, from a person dressed as a tramp pushing along a pram full of rubbish, to someone fishing in the street down a drainhole. You can use any sort of prop to help you – for example putting up a tent in the street and getting inside it. The leaders go off into the given area thirty minutes before the young people, who have been kept in a separate room so that they couldn't see what the leaders looked like.

When the youngsters are let loose they have to go out and find as many leaders as possible. They each have a pen and paper and have to get the signature of every leader they find. The game has a time limit of two hours, after which all the players meet up at a particular place to count heads. The person with the most names wins. When the young people think they recognise a leader, they ask a set question such as 'Have you seen my teddy bear, please?' If they have guessed right, a coded answer is given back such as 'Yes, it is in McDonalds having a milk shake.' (If the young people are wrong, the reply can be rather different!) As a safety measure, every young person has a letter explaining what is going on and a phone number for someone who is available to deal with any problems. It is a good idea to tell the police about the event a day before it is held. If the area is a 'problem' spot, pair up younger players with an older person.

INTER-CLUB EVENTS

It's a terrible waste not to meet and share activities with other local clubs, especially when funds are low. This can be done in very many ways, from football and table tennis matches to bath-tub races, discos and evening barbecues where everybody gets together and enjoys the fun. Mind you, with some groups things might not go totally smoothly, as club members can be very territorial, so a subtle approach is needed. After a few small evening and day trips you might be able to share resources on larger activities and excursions.

THEME DAY

If the days or evenings at the club seem to sink into the same old routine, why not liven them up by having a theme like a Hippie day, Punk day, Mod day or Roman day? Everyone has to dress up and act the part. The music has to be from the right era and some of the activities for the day are related to the theme, if possible. You could make it an open day for parents, so that they get a shock when they see their children in punk clothes or with coloured hair (that is, if they aren't punk already).

WALKABOUT

If it's a nice day and you have nothing special planned, get people to bring along a skateboard, bike, roller skates, go-kart, pogo stick, rugby ball or just themselves and go for a walk through your local park or heath. Simply keep on the move; play anything that comes into your head, and share all the equipment around. Have a rough route outlined, and just see what happens.

RATTLER

This is a fun game. All you need is a blindfold for every player except one, who needs to find an old tin can and place a few pebbles in it. The idea is for all the blindfolded people to grab the 'rattler', who is the person with the tin imitating the rattle of a snake. The rattler has to shake the pebbles every thirty seconds to let the others know where he/she is. When someone is caught, they then become the rattler. This can be played in confined spaces inside or outside. If you have trouble catching the rattler, blindfold them as well.

SHOE AND SOCK WARFARE

This game covers a large area; you can play it on the estates, but I think it will go down better in the parks and heaths where there is a lot of woodland and softer ground. The group can be anything from twenty people to about sixty. Divide the players into two teams, one with red arm-bands and the other with blue. The game starts from a fixed point, such as a park bench. One team has five minutes to run off and hide or avoid the other team, who will be following as soon as they are let loose. The idea is to hunt down and catch the members of the first team. When you catch someone you have to take their shoes and socks, and they, of course, will try to resist. If you do get their footwear off, they have to go back to base to wait for their shoes to arrive. After a while the teams can change roles. There are many tactics that can be used on both sides, such as going around in large groups or couples, and deciding whether to hide and wait or keep on the move. You should have agreed on an emergency whistle signal in case you need to call all the players back. If you play at night, it is best to stay in small groups and not run off by yourself, and it is a good idea to carry a torch to use after your shoes have been captured so that you can see where you are walking in your bare feet. You could vary the game so that you have more than two teams and each team has to catch as many people as possible from the others (count the shoes at the end). Even on grass you need to be careful that you do not cut your feet on broken glass or other rubbish. Take a first-aid kit just in case. Make sure that you return all shoes to base.

DUST PLAY

Most people make a point of avoiding dust, but on a hot dry day when you have very few clothes on and there is a pool to have a dip in afterwards to clean up, the idea is to find a piece of dusty land and with lots of friends play a game, such as football, that involves a lot of movement and kicks up the dust. You play the chosen game, but you all know that the main aim is to kick up as much dust as possible and get yourselves filthy. If there is a bit of a wind you can come on a downwind attack, kicking the dust over the person you are approaching. This is not a game for people who suffer from asthma.

THE SQUEEZE

The aim in this game is to get as many people as possible into a small place. See how many people you can get into a small cupboard, telephone box, public toilet or the old favourite – a mini. If you get stuck, rub soap around everyone to get them out.

TYRE KNOCK-OUT

This game is for groups of twenty or more. You need lots of tyres to roll – the more the merrier. In a hall or playground draw a chalk line at each end. Half the group stand behind one line and on the command 'GO' have to run to safety behind the opposite line. Meanwhile the other half of the team, from outside the running area, have to try to hit them as they run past by rolling the tyres at them, either all together or one at a time. (You could gang up on one person.) When you are hit, you are out. Once the remaining players are over the safety line, you call 'GO' again and they run back. This goes on until all the players are out, and then the two teams change places.

BALLOON RUGBY

This is great on a hot summer day when you need to cool off a little. Get a packet of balloons and fill them with with water. Arrange the space around you to form a pitch, and divide into two teams. The game is played like rugby, but with a water-filled balloon instead of a ball. The idea is to try to stay dry and make the other side burst the balloons so that they get wet. I'm not sure about kicking the balloon – sounds a bit suicidal.

INDOOR GAMES

Originally, when I was putting the ideas for this book together, I was going to call it something like *Outdoor Pursuits in the City.* But as I worked on it I felt uneasy about the name because it seemed to close off some potentially interesting areas. Some indoor activities are very much in line with the theme of the book, and some of the more artistic and imaginative ideas are in this category. The inside of a building is as much a part of a city as are the streets, and this book makes use of the creativity of the mind together with the players' environment. This chapter is short, because there is plenty of information elsewhere on indoor activities; but I wanted to include a few ideas to stimulate your imagination.

When I think of 'indoors', pictures come to mind of large church halls with a stage at one end, schools with lots of corridors and staircases, youth clubs with little rooms all over the place, or the small community centre in the middle of a council estate consisting of a single small room with a kitchen in one corner. Most of these places have tables, chairs, cupboards, stairs, floor space, brooms, mops, bins, and many more everyday objects that can be used as parts of a game. Having walls around you, thereby making a confined area, can be used as a positive element in a game. In some places, such as prisons, borstals and other institutions, players may not have much opportunity to get outside anyway.

Some activities normally played outside can be fun if brought inside the building – for example cricket nets in the hall, or playing a game of football with a sponge ball in a tiny room or even a cupboard. Hide and seek inside a building can stimulate a person to find the most amazing hideouts, such as under the sink or in the rubbish bin with the lid on! Climbing around the walls and tables without touching the floor is a real tactical task (as long as the furniture is solid and the caretaker approves). Lots of summer activities can be held inside, from running a jumble sale to a tiddlywinks competition. Indoors, people don't feel the need to throw themselves around like monkeys; many activities may be of a calmer nature but just as much fun, like a cooking exercise or a hammock-making and sleeping project. A sports fete or mini Olympics could be held using the building and its objects for lots of silly events, with a tape in the background playing 'Chariots of Fire'. Anything is acceptable, so long as it's not dangerous, doesn't break things and is properly run.

Being able to control the environment, like the lights and the heating, is another factor that can be used to advantage. Many activities described in other chapters of this book could be tried indoors. One of the main lessons I have learnt from bitter experience (and the caretaker chasing me all over the building) is that light bulbs, windows and door hinges seem to break easily. So it's a good idea to adapt some of the equipment being used, and make sure you don't use anything which will mark the caretaker's pride and joy – the highly polished wooden floor. Common sense, planning and consultation are essential.

THE GAMES

INDOOR JAMMING

If you remember, in infants' school you used to line up lots of empty milk bottles and fill them with different amounts of water, then hit them with a stick to get a nice sound. Each one had a different pitch because of the various water levels. In this activity you don't stop at milk bottles, but go into the kitchen and get out lots of different pots and pans and whatever else you can find that might make a good noise. You can hit them with all sorts of objects to vary the sounds, from knives and forks to wire egg whisks. Why not make a tape recording of the session? Give the neighbours lots of cotton wool!

DRESSING-UP EVENING

Some people love to dress up, so why not have an evening when everyone has to do it? Decide on a particular night, and lay on a few bits of food and some light music. This might exclude some people who, like me, have no sense of dress, but probably not too many, as some might have expensive clothes they want to show off, while others have a real talent for looking great wearing things they have picked up at a jumble sale. You may want to come looking really bizarre, or dress down for a giggle. The group should know each other to set the right atmosphere, and do be careful not to make the poorer members feel bad.

MOP AND BROOM RACE

This game is very devious and can be played at the end of the day in the large hall or yard. There are many variations; one is to get together enough brooms for the players to have one each. They all line up at one end with the brushes on the floor, then rush to the other end without the broom leaving the ground. You could have relays or play follow the leader, where you line up side by side so that all the broom heads are together; the person on the left is the leader, so if they're running along and turn to the right, so do the others, trying to keep the broom heads together. The leader can vary the speed, direction and objects to go around. When you've tried it with the brooms, you can do it again with damp mops. It's a good way to clean up at the end of the day.

SNEAKER PILE

This indoor game needs a minimum of about thirty players. Get the group all together in one room and get everyone to take off their sneakers or shoes. Take all the footwear into another room and mix them up in one large pile. On the word 'GO' all the players have to rush into the room and rummage through the pile. The first one with both their own shoes back on their feet wins, the next is second, and so on. It's harder than you think, as there will be lots of shoes that are very alike and some players might not be able to tell which are theirs. Can you imagine how many white sneakers there will be? The game cannot finish until everyone has their own shoes on, as people might have trouble walking home.

INDOOR SPORTS FETE

People often organise fetes, but this one is held indoors and consists only of sports - silly sports. It could be just for fun, or open to the public for fund-raising. Arrange lots of daft events that involve tiddlywinks, wet sponges, throwing balls into buckets, press-ups and so on. The one-leg, standing-start long jump may give you an idea of the type of events to organise. You will probably need a refreshment area after all this energetic work. With good publicity and ideas, it could turn out to be a terrific fete.

INDOOR TIDDLYWINKS

Don't laugh - some people take their tiddlywinks very seriously and go in for national competitions and world records. Mind you, this version is for fun, or at most a doughnut wager. First you get some tiddlywinks, and then set a course. It may start downstairs and go all over the building. You have to flip the tiddlywinks around the set route - under the table, up the stairs, around the toilet basin, over the cat, and so on until you get to the finish line. Players go round one at a time. You could also have a mini athletic track marked out with different events, such as the high jump or long jump; you may even do the 10-metre dash. The winner gets a doughnut. If you don't like doughnuts, send it to me.

SCRATCHING JAM SESSION

Here you need some fancy equipment: a couple of old mono record players found on a junk stall or in one of the members' houses, and a tape recorder. Give the players a set time to jam, and then record their session. They have the basic two record players, and anything else they want to use to make sounds, such as a snooker cue, a chair or whatever. If you don't know what scratching is, shame on you! It's where you move the record fast and slow with your hand as it plays forwards and backwards, making peculiar sounds. With the other object like the chair they put a pad on one bit and use that to alter the record. This might seem a bit of a strange pastime, but when it is done well it sounds great.

MINIATURE SPORTS

This is a very simple idea which can be a lot of fun. Take a sport that is normally played in a large area, and play it in a small one. A simple example would be football. Find a small yard or room and get lots of players into it, dividing them into two teams with goals as for a normal game. You could try playing in a large broom cupboard – perhaps with just five a side. Basketball or netball could also be fun with only a few inches between players. Avoid games like baseball and cricket, because they are too dangerous. But how about a mixed-sex rugby match?

THREADING THE ROPE

This is a fun game to try when you're stuck indoors, and it's a good way to get to know each other. All you need is a long piece of rope – a dry climbing rope will do fine. Everyone lines up side by side, with the rope at one end of the line. The first person has to thread the rope through some of their clothes, for example up one trouser leg and down the other. The next person continues threading the rope, perhaps through their sleeves this time. This goes on along the line until the rope has passed through everyone. It's a great ice-breaker! (And if the rope is dirty, it will probably be a neck-breaker for the person whose idea it was!)

GLASS FACE PHOTOGRAPHY

This sounds a bit like a violent scene at pub closing time – well it's not! The idea is simply to clean a sheet of glass, such as a window or door, and squash your face against one side making the silliest face you can. On the other side of the glass someone with a camera takes photos of your expressions. The film can be black and white so you can develop the prints yourselves, or slides so you can project on to a large screen. You can have themes, such as monster faces or drunks' faces. Make sure the glass is strong and not a cheap, thin glass that might break when you press your face against it. Mind you, there is nothing you can do if you're so ugly that you break the glass just by looking at it!

ROOM CLEAR-OUT

Imagine you have a room full of people doing different things all around the place. Tell them to stop whatever they are doing, explain to them that there is a dangerous chemical or animal in the room and that they have to get up off the floor. They then have to get out of the room without touching the floor; they can help each other, but if they touch the floor at any time they are out. Use chairs, tables, radiators and anything else that will make a bridge or an escape route. Make sure you have permission, and that the chairs and other supports are strong enough.

STAIRCASE FITNESS

If you belong to a group that has training sessions, or you just want to get fit, there are many ways of doing this. A general fitness exercise to get the lungs heaving and the heart thumping and, of course, to strengthen the legs is to find a staircase in a block of flats and simply run up and down. You will need to build up slowly, because if you run up twenty flights of stairs straight away you could damage your knees. So warm up first and gradually increase the length of the exercise. Work hard going up the stairs, but ease off coming down as there is the possibility of twisting an ankle or falling.

TABLE CLIMBING

For this game you need a strong table. Start by getting on top of the table, then try to climb all the way under it and up the other side without touching the floor or anything else for support. If you manage this, try it from different directions, then progress to other articles of furniture, such as chairs and desks. Make sure they are strong and will

not fall over when you are half-way around. This is the sort of game that is ideal when everyone is sitting around doing nothing. Someone suddenly starts playing it, and although they might initially get some strange looks from the others, within five minutes everybody wants a go. They might fall off, but they will keep on trying. Life's funny sometimes.

SOCK SLIDING

This is an indoor game that is terrific fun to play, although it can be very exhausting. You need a room which has a wooden floor that is always highly polished. These can often be found in school buildings or church halls. At first, players simply take off their shoes and start sliding around. When they have mastered this, you can introduce other ideas such as sock sliding football or basketball. There's also Murder Ball, where the players have to hit each other with the ball, and you could try sliding limbo. When you are tired and decide to call it a day, have a look at the colour of your socks.

BLINDFOLDED PAIRS

In this game divide the group into pairs; one partner has to wear a blindfold, while the other gives directions. These could be very simple, such as asking them to walk around the room avoiding the chairs, or something more complicated like getting them to put up a tent or make a sandwich. The sighted partner must not touch the blindfolded person except in an emergency; all instructions and directions have to be verbal. After the blind person has done the given task, the partners change roles. This is good fun, although people can get irritable when they discover they can't do things, and start to cheat or give up. Some people try this just to find out what it's like to be blind, although of course there is no real comparison.

MAKING BREAD

This makes a good indoor activity in winter. We often take the sliced supermarket loaf for granted, whereas years ago most people would have known how to make their own bread. First, plan what you need and set an evening in the club to make and bake bread – assuming you have a cooker. Bring some cheese or bacon, and at the end of the evening you can have a little food party. There are many different sorts of bread you can bake. You could even study how people used to make their own kilns out of stone, and see if you can build one outside to use for your own baking.

MEMBERS' MEAL

This idea makes my mouth water just thinking about it. A nice activity once a year is for the club to have an evening where the members plan and make a large feast for themselves and invite the staff and parents. Christmas is a good time, but it's up to you to decide. Organise all the members to do different jobs – some do the shopping, some cook, some lay the tables and so on. You could have a few speeches, perhaps some entertainment, and a little music afterwards.

COOKING PARTY

In a small club it could be possible to have one evening a week when members take turns to cook for the whole group. You could make up a rota for the coming month, with two or three in each cooking group. It is surprising how many boys and girls have never cooked even for themselves, let alone anyone else – often simply because their parents won't let them loose in the kitchen. Some of these people will probably not want to be part of a cooking group, so you'll have to think of a good way of persuading them – for example, no-one is allowed to eat unless they put their name down to cook. (Be careful they don't eat for a few weeks and then go missing on their cook night!) With success, a lot of confidence can be built up from this activity. It might be a good idea to go for a safe 'first try' by choosing a couple of young people that you know can cook, to get it off to a good start.

TASTING PARTY

One of the most important things in life is eating; well, for some of us anyway. It's something we have to do to stay healthy and active, so why not make it more interesting by trying out a few different tastes? Our senses of sight and smell affect the way we feel about what we taste. The idea here is to cut out sight by blindfolding all the players, and to block out the sense of smell with some cotton wool. A couple of nonplayers set up a variety of foods and drinks in another room. The players come in and carefully move around, sampling the food and drink and saying what they think it is after each tasting. When everyone has sampled everything, take off the blindfolds and let the players see the food and drink (if there is any left). Some foods might be in unusual combinations, such as small sausages in jelly, or you could dye all the food different colours so that it looks peculiar even though it still tasted good. After the game you all polish off whatever is left.

MINIBUS FINGER SPELLING

Finger-spelling the deaf alphabet is a good way to while away travelling time in the minibus. Your local organization for the deaf will have the cards to learn the alphabet from, and it doesn't take long to learn the letters. You can then progress to spelling your name and 'reading' other people's sentences.

PUNISHMENT TASK

Yes, this does sound like something out of the dark ages, but some people actually enjoy punishing themselves or other people. The idea is to play a game where you all have to write down on individual bits of paper some really mad and stupid ideas for things to do. All the pieces of paper are then folded up and placed in a box or hat like a raffle-ticket draw. Each player may put up to three different ideas in the hat, on separate bits of paper with their initials on the back. One at a time players pull out a ticket and have to perform the task written on it. When they have finished, the next player has a pick. The tasks have to be possible, otherwise it gets too silly. The following are some ideas for tasks.

1. Carry a table around the block.
2. Put the rubbish bin on your head.

3 Piggy-back carry the heaviest person in the room up one flight of stairs.

4 Pick your nose in front of everyone.

Yes, it's sick – but it takes all sorts to make the world. If a player doesn't carry out the task, they are out of the game.

COCK FIGHTING

This game used to be played in schools in the 1930s as part of a pool gala in a swimming pool, but it could also be played over a large mud pit (or even inside a gym using benches). You need a long, strong plank to go from one side of the water or mud to the other. Split the group into two equal teams, which then line up at opposite ends of the plank. Have the smallest people at the front and increase in size to the biggest at the back. One person at a time from each team has to cross the plank with their arms folded. The problem comes when they meet in the middle: they have to fight until one is victorious and the other is in the water or mud. The only way you can fight is to lift your leg against the other person's leg and try to catch them off balance; the action isn't a kick, but rather a shove. When successful a player carries on to the other side, then the next two from each team try to cross. This goes on until every person has had a go. The team with the most across is the winner, or they could try to cross again until the whole of the opposing team has been wiped out.

HIDE AND SEEK (INDOORS)

This is the same as any game of hide and seek, but players must not leave the building. As a result you have to hide in one of the rooms, corridors, halls, cupboards or anywhere else in the building. You will be surprised at what you can find to hide in, even if it means getting dirty or a bit smelly. Some hide and some seek, and after a set time a whistle is blown to call everyone together to change places. When the game is over, count how many were caught on each side; the one with the least wins.

SUMO WRESTLING

This is an oriental type of wrestling usually performed by very large men, but here we use lighter lads and introduce women. First draw a circle on the floor with chalk, about 10 feet wide. Then wrap a jumper around your waist like a nappy. Two people enter the circle and try to throw each other out; both feet have to be out of the circle for it to count as out. The winner stays in the circle to take on the next challenger. If you have soft land or soft mats to play on, it makes for a more comfortable landing. The jumper around the waist is for grabbing. A bow before and after each bout adds to the oriental flavour.

ORGANISING YOUR OWN TRIP

Sometimes staff do a little too much for club members, which is fine when they're young, but when they start to get a bit more responsible let them have a go at organising a trip themselves, using staff if they need to. A good idea might be a day trip to the seaside. They will have to find out what station to go to, or ask if they can use the club transport and borrow a member of staff, and they will need to do the costing for fuel and work out the timetable. Another possibility could be a weekend camp, where the problems to be solved might be more complex. Some trips may not require an adult to go along, but members should always get permission and let staff know of their plans.

MAKING AND BUILDING

Making and building things can be very satisfying, and a lot of fun can be had during the process of getting the materials, putting them together and finishing them off. There are so many things you can make that I can only scratch the surface in this chapter. Making and building are very creative activities, because you are thinking and working all the time. They are also constructive activities, rather than destructive ones; for some kids this would be a welcome change, *if* you can capture their interest.

This sort of activity can be carried out inside or outside. It could be making something small in the arts and crafts session, or doing a job of work outside the club on a large scale, like cleaning the brickwork or laying a new garden path. You could be both in and out, converting a window-pane into stained glass. Growing flowers or vegetables and displaying them or making a meal from them also come into this category.

There are very many things you can make – toys, tools, murals, clothes, furniture, play-structures, huts and homes, ornaments, go-karts, rafts, things that fly. Then there are large projects, such as customising real cars in the workshop (with an expert around), or more simple ideas, such as spraying a push-bike a different colour or making a doorbell. When I was at school, as a school project we made the Dalek commander which was used in the actual *Doctor Who* programme. The year before, a group had made a real hovercraft which worked and was lots of fun floating around the playground.

Some things that you would like to buy may be too expensive, difficult to get, or simply the wrong size. So why not try to make them? It might be clothes, a toy like a pogo stick, or even a pair of stilts. Working as a group, you could make lots of different things which can be sold to help raise funds for the club or some other worthwhile cause.

The thing I make best is a mess!

THE GAMES

UMBRELLA MAKING

Yes, it's another one of those days when it won't stop raining, and the youngsters are looking a little down. Have a look around the club and see what is lying around, then make an umbrella in the comfort of the clubhouse and go out into the rain and see if it works. If you want to have a bit of fun and make it into a competition, you could judge it on some or all of the following ideas.

1 Speed: the fastest to make one
2 Most original concept
3 Most artistic design
4 The one that lasts longest
5 The one that best keeps the water out

You can choose a theme to base the design on – a Chinese umbrella, one for four people, or one with silly accessories like hanging teapots and a miniature gas cooker (in case you're stuck at the bus stop for a long time!). Even if it's not raining, you can still make umbrellas and use the hosepipe to supply the water.

MAKE YOUR OWN CLOTHES

There are many different ways in which you can do this, ranging from the normal to the totally ridiculous. You could have a project where a group of young people design, buy the material, make and finally wear some articles of clothing they like and would wear on a night out. Or you can hold a session with a theme such as tramps, or bits of a kitchen and its utensils, where you use any old materials and other objects you find lying around – so if you want to incorporate a dustbin lid into the costume design, go right ahead. If you have a sewing machine, great; if not, you can use safety pins or a needle and thread.

TOY PARACHUTES

If you find an unwanted sheet of polythene blowing around or have some bin liners and string you could make some toy parachutes varying between 1 foot and 6 feet in size. The idea is to attach small weights or objects to them and drop them from heights. Remember that these are *not* for people to jump with – a parachute is a highly intricate piece of specialist equipment which can only do its job in jumps from at least 1000 feet high. Join a parachute club if you are interested in the real thing.

MONO STILT

This stilt is very simple to make, but it can take a lot of practice to master it. All you need are three strong pieces of wood or tree branches – two the same length of about 5 feet and another about 3 feet 6 inches in length. Assemble the pieces like the letter A, with the crossbar sticking out about 6 inches either side. Tie it all together very firmly; it is now ready for use. You stand on the outside bits of the crossbar, hold on to the top of the A piece, and wobble along. After a while you can get quite good at it and climb slopes and small steps, or even try a 360° turn on one leg.

HOT-AIR BALLOON

I'm not sure what the aviation rules are about real, full-size hot-air balloons with baskets underneath them full of people. But here we are talking about a small balloon between 2 feet and 10 feet in size. You will need to investigate all the possible materials, and find a simple but *safe* method of getting the warm air into the balloon – one of the new hot-air paint strippers might be a good idea. Always have a line attached to the balloon at one end and the ground at the other to keep it under control. If you are using fire rather than a power electric fan, be very careful of the obvious fire risk and burns. The fire must *never* go up with the balloon in case it breaks loose and lands on a house. You could try to lift small objects around the yard or playground. With a lot of work, and making sure you respect the regulations, you should be able to make a very respectable balloon. After your toy project, why not write to a real ballooning club and organise a flight?

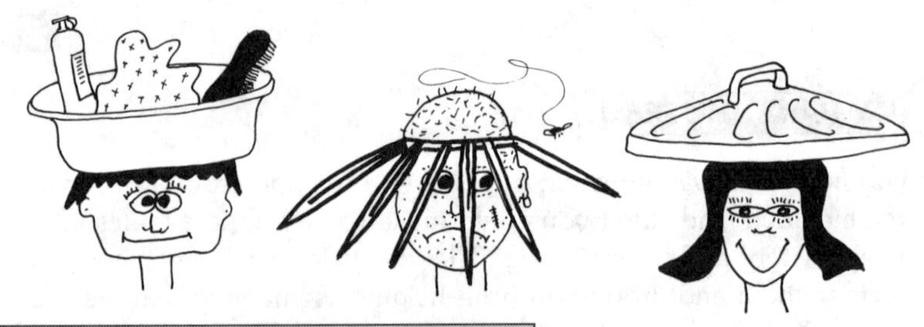

PLAYGROUND BOARD SAILING

Not every school or youth club has a fleet of windsurfers or water space available on their doorstep. So why not find an old door, put some wheels on it and use an old bed sheet to make a sail? This is a very basic and stable board, but as you progress you can make more advanced boards that can turn and move upwind. Look in the shops to see how professionals make theirs, and try to do the same cheaply and simply. As you start to go faster you will need to wear protective clothes like knee and elbow pads, and you must wear a crash helmet like skateboarders. How about trying a double board?

MUSCLE-POWERED VEHICLE

In this activity you make a vehicle that can run on roads, snow or water. It can be a very simple project or a very sophisticated one taking weeks to complete. Unlike go-karts where you are pushed, roll down hills or use the wind to move along, this vehicle has to be a mechanical one that uses the muscle power of its riders. This might mean converting a push-bike, or you can devise some other method of propulsion. Ride your vehicle for fun or have a race as part of a competition against other local clubs, or even use it as part of a sponsored fund-raising event for charity.

PAPER PLANE MAKING AND FLYING

Lots of people make paper planes at some time in their lives and fly them across a room (often at a teacher, if I remember right!) Working as a group you could make lots of planes of all shapes and sizes, using paper and thin cardboard; make giant planes and fly them locally to see if the design works. A good place to try them out is from a balcony on the top floor of a block of flats. If there is a good wind, organise a competition to see whose flies the furthest.

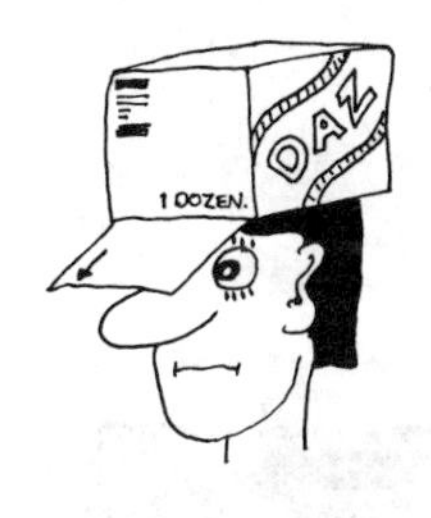

HAT MAKING

There are many reasons for wearing a hat. You may want to keep off the rain or sun, cover up a bald patch, or just look super cool. You can make a hat to suit a theme. For example, for a rainy-day theme you could have an outrageous hat the size of an umbrella, or a contraption that not only keeps the rain off but also has a drainpipe that catches and stores the water. You could make a hat for a windy day that has a fan on the front to make a breeze. Of course, you could simply have a fairly normal hat made out of woven straw or reeds. There are many other types of hat you can make, for example for a pantomime or dressing-up session, out of papier mâché or objects found around the house (paper bags or plates, lampshades, tea towels, etc.) You may decide to hold your own version of Ascot and all wear a hat to a party or on a day trip.

FASHION SHOW

The idea here is organise a whole evening which incorporates a fashion show. Start the evening with a light meal for everyone; then stage the fashion show, followed by a disco. The fashion show can have different sections so that some people dress up in really fancy gear and others dress down and a bit way out. Have some music and lights as the models walk up and down the catwalk. If you like, you can have some judges to choose the best and the worst dressed.

JAMAICAN BOXWOOD BIKE

This bike construction is like a boxwood go-kart made up of odd bits and pieces and some wheels, but rather than using four wheels as for a normal kart, you use only two like a motor bike. There are no pedals or any other form of propulsion apart from your own legs. Like *The Flintstones* on TV you sit on the vehicle and run along with your legs,

rolling when you feel like it. You can make some sort of brake if you like, but just putting your feet on the ground is enough. You have a lump of wood as the handlebars, which are just for holding on to and not for steering. These 'bikes' are very basic and primitive, but one hell of a lot of fun. I can imagine half a dozen adults on them, rattling around the town centre on a pub crawl or sponsored event.

OCHO RIOS BEAD MAKING

Ocho Rios is a place in Jamaica that has many different types of fruit trees, and the fruits themselves have seeds of all shapes and sizes, from minute pips to coconut shells. It is also close to the sea, and there is a good supply of differently shaped seashells washed up on the beaches. The locals make various pieces of jewellery, beads and wristbands out of the many combinations of seeds and shells.

The aim here is to collect lots of seeds that you find in the city in the food you eat, like apples, melons, oranges and so on, and to make anything you like out of them. If you are near a beach, you should be able to get hold of some shells as well. To be really different you could use all sorts of found objects to make things with, like shirt buttons, sequins, nuts, bolts and washers. Once you are good at it, you could start making all sorts of jewellery, and perhaps even have a stall in your local flea market.

KITE BUILDING AND FLYING

Building and flying kites is a pastime that has been around for hundreds of years. Kites have been used for many different functions, from transportation to a wartime aid where someone goes up with a kite to see if there are any ships over the horizon. Here I want to concentrate on the fun aspect. You could simply get out that old kite from under the bed and fly it on a windy day on a local hill or from a top balcony of some nearby flats. If you don't already have a kite, start a project to build one to your own design out of black plastic bin liners, thin gardening sticks and waterproof tape; there are lots of books on kite making to help you. There are very many different sorts you can make, from mini pocket-size kites to giant ones that need two of you to hold them down.

You could use a kite, while wearing rollerskates or sitting in a small boat, to pull you along. Or how about having a go at lifting an object off the ground, by getting lots of kites all connected up to the object? If there is a large piece of flat ground near you, like a car park (empty), you could sit on your home-made go-kart and use the kite as an engine to pull you along, steering with your feet to move around the obstacles. But quite apart from all these ideas, it can be a really enjoyable thing just to sit on a park bench on the top of a hill, flying a kite and meditating.

MECHANICS FOR FUN

Some people love mechanics, and some really hate it. Usually, if you need to do something mechanical to an engine it's because something has gone wrong, and it always seems to be in the cold weather when your hands are going to freeze. If you have a few tools and a bit of space to use for a few weeks, why not search local waste land or ask a local garage for an old engine for the club members to play with? This won't cost you anything – there are normally lots of unwanted engines around. Ideally, the project would be to take the engine apart and then put it back together again. Two-stroke motorbike engines are probably the easiest to start with. You could either buy a manual for that particular engine, or make little drawings as you take it to bits. If you find that you can't put it back together, at least you won't be in trouble with anyone. Mechanics are not as difficult as most people think, and it might give you confidence and valuable knowledge for the future so that you can do small jobs on your own vehicle. Then again, it might turn you off for life!

MAKING MUSICAL INSTRUMENTS

Earlier in the book we adapted objects to improvise an instrument such as pots and pans to make a drum kit, but here the idea is to *make* your own instrument. It can be a model of a standard instrument, such as a flute or bagpipes, or you could come up with a new idea using strings, wind or whatever. If there is a group making a few instruments, maybe a concert at the end would be fun.

BAMBOO VIOLIN

When I was in the Caribbean, I met a man selling bamboo violins that he had made. They do not look like violins but sound very similar and are played in the same way with a stick cut from the bamboo. They have only a few strings, so you can learn to play them very quickly. The bamboo is in one complete piece about 3 inches in diameter and about 14 inches long. The strings are a part of the side. Carve the side

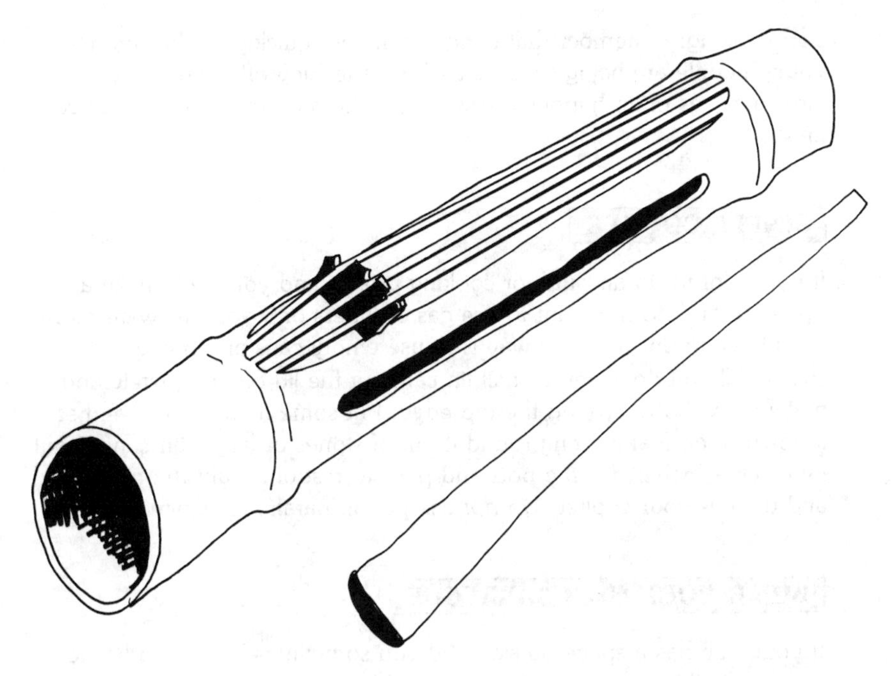

to allow the sound to come out, and use a prop of wood to tighten up the strings. The diagram shows what it should look like. You can buy bamboo from some shops, but if you can't find any, ring up a zoo and see where they get theirs from.

COOKING OUT

Cooking outside is great fun, and food tastes especially good in the open by the comfort of a warm fire. First you need heat: this can be a camping stove or, better still, an open fire. Always make sure you have clean hands when cooking and handling food. A simple thing to start with is a cup of tea. Then you can move on to baked potatoes, sausages on sticks, fried eggs, beans, and don't forget some vegiburgers for the vegetarians, because they are often left out. You can cook some foods in their cans, or use bricks and arrange the fire so that you can use pots and pans. Do not use rubber or other rubbish, and make sure the wood in the fire doesn't have paint on it, as this will harm the food and create fumes. Wait until the fire burns down to a glow, and then start cooking; remember that things cook very quickly. Make sure the young people are being sensible and not sneaking off making fires elsewhere, as often happens. Always put the fire out properly after you finish.

SIMPLE COOKER

If you want to do an outdoor cooking project and you can't make an open fire and do not want to use gas cylinders or if you just want more rings to cook on, a simple way is to use empty cans and methylated spirits. All you do is get a small tin can, cut the lid off completely and make a few holes around the top edge. Put some meths into it and set it down, then make a ring round it out of stones or larger tin cans about two inches higher, for the pots and pans to rest on. Light the meths, and there is your cooker. Do *not* use petrol, paraffin or white spirit.

BUILD YOUR OWN BARBECUE

If your club has a space outside and you sometimes have a barbecue, why not build your own? Make it out of bricks, or use a large metal drum like they do in Jamaica and other countries. Once you've made it, you will have to practise cooking on it; there is quite an art to running a good barbecue. Build a cover to use in bad weather. Barbecues can be fun when it's raining – for example under a shelter in the school playground.

CLUB ODD JOBS

I say odd jobs, but they can in fact be major ones. Some members might actually enjoy doing a few tasks around the club, like cleaning the mini-bus if you have one, a bit of repair work outside on that fallen wall, or crazy paving you've been meaning to lay for the last five years. Most will do it just for fun, or you could take them for a day trip in return. Mind you, I can think of a few people in my own club who would collapse with laughter if I even suggested the idea.

BRIGHTEN IT UP

If the building you use looks a hundred years old and is in a dull-looking street, see if you can find ways of cheering it up. Perhaps you could paint your old hut or windows and doors, or create a mural on a wall. (There are lots of books on murals that will give you some ideas.) Or how about making a new sign for the club which is colourful and welcoming to new members?

RESTORATION PROJECT

Cities are full of very old and historic sites, ranging from houses, roads, churches, parks, canals, bridges and graveyards to old gas lamp-posts. In many cases, societies have been formed in order to preserve these sites, and you can contact these and arrange to go and help to restore them. If not, you could start your own project, if you can find something worth saving. It doesn't have to be a big project; you could just work on a part of your own building, like redoing the pointing on the brickwork, turning the bit of waste land at the back of the club into a garden, or even giving the club a bit of a face lift to make it look more welcoming. You can have a lot of fun working on these projects getting really tired and dirty, but when that nice hot cup of tea comes out and you stand back and look at the results of your efforts it all seems worth while.

PLANT A TREE

It's tough for most *people* to survive in the city, let alone a tree. If your club has a suitable area, or you find somewhere locally that would be a nice spot, and if you can get permission to plant a tree, why not try it? There is a lot more involved than you think. Besides getting permission, you will have to decide on the type of tree, read up on growing it, make sure that in twenty years' time the roots aren't going to cause damage, and be prepared to look after it for the first couple of years. Your biggest problem will be protecting if from the public. Years later, when it's as tall as the other trees around, you will be really proud of it. You could even give it a name.

CAR BODYWORK

If you happen to come across an old car lying around or, more likely, one of the members of staff has an old banger with a few dents in it (which is not unusual for a youth worker), then maybe with their consent you can run a project on doing up the bodywork. It's not as hard as people think, if you read up on how to do it and start on a small dent first. I'm sure the results will be lovely!

WORK IN THE DARK

In this game you need a very dark room and, inside it, some objects that need to be put together or worked on in some way, such as a box frame made out of scaffold tubes and joints, or some other form of assembly job. Each person has to do the task in the dark, and the one who does it the fastest wins.

DRAWING CLASS

If you have some young people in the group who are interested in art and drawing but have only worked in the classroom or club building, try taking them wider afield to some more exciting places. Most people are very self-conscious about trying to draw in public, but when you try it you find it's not as bad as you thought. The city is full of things to draw: market places, canals, railway stations, people, museums, car scrap heaps, zoos, streets, parks, night scenes, etc. All you need is a board, paper, rubber and something to draw with. Being part of a group helps to overcome any embarrassment at drawing in the streets, and can also help you to see a lot more than you normally do.

THATCHED HUT

If the council have trimmed the trees and left the branches and twigs lying around for ages, use them to make a thatched house by weaving them together into a dome shape with a door and even a window in it. To start with you need to make a circle on the earth with a stick. Place about six to ten firm branches sticking up from points around the circle, and tie them together at the top. Then weave the rest in and out of these to make the walls. You can have any shape you like, and you could cover it with leaves for warmth or camouflage.

BLINDFOLD TENT CONSTRUCTION

In this game you have to try to put up a tent while blindfolded. You'll be surprised at the amount of fun you can have trying this, and how much you can learn about how or how not to do it. If there are lots of people playing, get a few tents and split the group into teams of four. Have one sighted person supervising to keep an eye out for cheats. The following are some variations.

1 One person per tent.
2 Four per tent, and they are allowed to talk.
3 Four per tent, but they are not allowed to talk or make any sounds; they can communicate by touch only.
4 Five per tent, one sighted and the other four blindfolded. The sighted player cannot touch any part of the tent or any of the other players; they can only give verbal help.
5 Twenty blindfolded people per tent.

Have a good look afterwards with the blindfolds off and see how well or how badly you have done. Then put the blindfolds back on and try to pack away the tent as neatly as possible.

FOOTWEAR

We spoiled city people who, when we need something, can go to the corner shop and buy almost anything, take too many things for granted. Footwear is a typical example. I was in Mexico where everyone is small, and my own shoes having worn out I unsuccessfully visited a dozen or so shops to try to buy some in my size. I soon realised that if I didn't wish to walk around in bare feet, I would have to make my own. What a terrific project it would be to make your own footwear, from the serious variety to the ridiculous. The only ways I have seen city people attempting to rearrange their footwear are by spraying them a different colour, or putting polythene bags over them when it is snowing. Reading up on other cultures' methods from around the world could be a useful way of getting ideas. Often, reeds and leather are used in very simple ways that work very well. Discarded material like rubber tyres can be worked into hard-wearing and attractive sandals.

GROUND AND WALL MARKINGS

People have used the ground and walls for making marks on for thousands of years. The markings may tell a story, give a message, or explain a history or culture of a past race. They may be a secret code, a game or simply a nice picture.

We use marks every day, for example the white lines in the middle of the road or to stop us at a junction. We see graffiti on walls or bridges as we pass by, and when we cross the road we use the black and white markings of a pedestrian crossing. Tramps used to leave secret signs chalked on the road or outside houses to tell each other of a vicious dog or a friendly, generous owner. In a busy tourist area you may find a pavement artist busking for money. Marks can be found both inside buildings and outside on the streets or playgrounds. They may be permanently painted for regular use, or drawn with chalk which lasts only until people's feet have worn it out or the rain has washed it away. A mark may simply be a footprint in the soil or sand. I've even seen marks on grass that wash off with the first rain and do not harm the soil.

So there is a wide range of uses and methods of marking, and endless variations to adapt for games. A good example of an indoor game using marks is stepping stones and boiling water. Lots of chalk circles are drawn all over the floor to be used as stepping stones over imaginary boiling water. A street game could be a treasure hunt, with clues marked on the walls that you have to follow to find the rewards.

Once at college someone played a joke on the Principal. They painted footmarks which started from the Principal's office and as you followed them they went to the bar, then the toilet, then over the grass through the fountain, up the side of the building and back into the Principal's office window. It was very funny to watch everyone following the steps. Nobody knew who had done it, but the best thing about it was that it was all cleaned up without any damage or marks left. (How they got up the wall is still a mystery!)

Depending on the game, you have to decide whether to play it on soft or hard ground. If there is lots of jumping and falling over, the softer the ground the better. You may not need to make your own marks: they may already be there, like damp patches after a rainstorm or the normal pitch markings used for team games which you can use in a different way. Both large and small groups can make use of markings, in games ranging from bridge cross to hopscotch. For a night game, you can make marks that reflect as a torch shines on to them, or a fluorescent marker could be used. When playing on any type of surface, always look over the area first for broken glass or any nasty sticks poking out of the ground. Always clear up after the game is finished.

THE GAMES

CROCKERY TRAIL

This is a team game played with markings in sand or dry soil. If you have twenty or more players, divide the group into teams of five. Each team has a plastic breakfast bowl which is put into a hole in the sand. All the teams line up behind their bowls, and equal, measured amounts of water are poured into each bowl by the leader.

The leader then draws markings in the sand with a stick. If these are lines, the players have to walk along all of them and come back while carrying the bowl; if it is a circle, players must walk one circuit, keeping on the line. On the word 'GO' the first member of each team has to pick up the bowl very carefully so as not to spill any water, and then complete the course. All the teams have to complete the same course, so if someone is already on one line then the next player goes to another. When the first player comes back they must replace the bowl in the hole for the next team member to pick up. This goes on until all the players have walked the course. If any markings get wiped out, the leader redraws them while the game is still in motion. The aim is not to finish first but rather to have the most water at the end, so you do need to measure it.

BRIDGE CROSSING

This game needs a section of land inside or out that will take chalk marks. The theme is a bridge that has to be crossed by one group, this being the only bridge across the river for miles. The problem is that there is another group that doesn't want them to cross.

From a bird's eye view, draw a simple bridge crossing a river. Divide the group into two equal teams; one has to try to cross the bridge, while the other has to defend it. The defending team stands on the bridge; the others are near it behind a line, and their goal is a similar line on the other side of the bridge. Once you leave the first line you cannot go back over it for safety, and anyone who puts two feet in the river is out. The defenders have to try to stop the others by pushing them into the river, but if they fall in themselves, they drown and are out. There is no time limit, as it is a fight to the death. If some get across and there are still some defenders on the bridge, you could either count how many are left or let the remaining players try to cross again and again until one group is knocked out. Have a short rest after the game and start again, changing team roles.

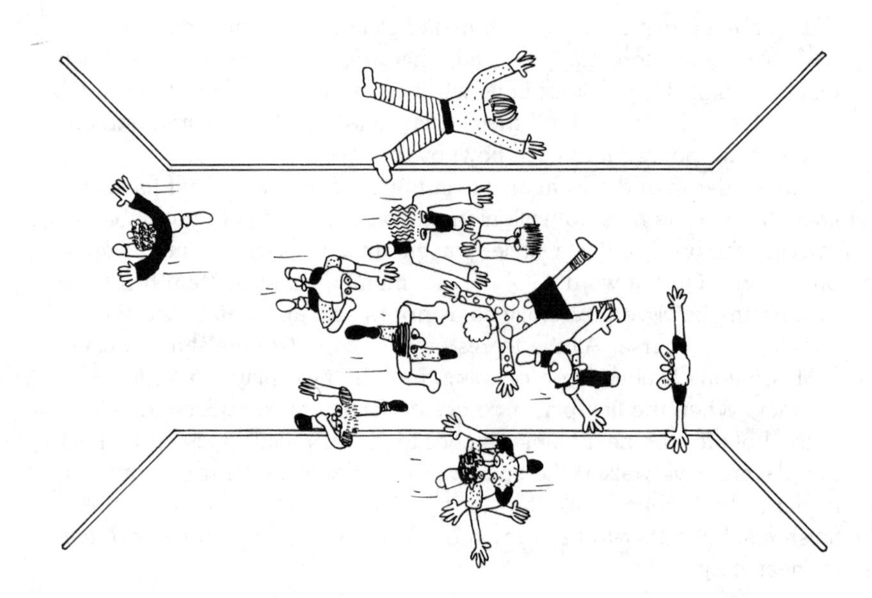

HOPSCOTCH

I just want to mention hopscotch in passing, as there are so many different variations around the world that it would take for ever to write them all down - and there are already whole books on the subject anyway. For those who are not sure what hopscotch is, it is a game where players mark out a pattern of squares with chalk and have to throw a stone into one of the squares. If they get it into a box then they have to hop in different ways up the pattern, pick up the stone and bring it back. One variation I saw in Spain is that instead of throwing the stone, you have to hop around the pattern, kicking the stone into each box without putting the other foot down. There are various different patterns, different ways of hopping and different ways of playing, so I will stop now.

TARGET LANDINGS

In this game you need to play in an area which has lots of stones or objects to throw. It could be done indoors, but it is better on sand or soil. At a distance, place a sheet about 1 foot square on the ground. If there is a slight wind you can weight the paper with stones at each corner. The idea is to have ten stones each and, one at a time, throw a stone so that it lands on the paper. It must stay there to count. If it bounces off, hard luck; work on a different throwing technique. The one with the most landings wins, and a new game starts when all the stones have been thrown. If it is too difficult, shorten the distance you have to throw. If one stone knocks another off, that is also hard luck and is not counted. (Some games just aren't fair!) You could play in pairs, trying to knock each other's stones off and keep your own stones on. It helps if you mark your stones with your initials or a distinctive colour.

GOLD POT

This game is normally played with marbles, but I think it adapts well to tennis balls or footballs. You need an area close to a wall with soil or sandy ground in front of it, and one ball for each player. Mark a triangle in the loose ground about 6 feet in front of the wall. Something nice has to be put into the triangle, such as a Mars bar. The idea is to start at a set distance away, and one at a time you either throw, roll or kick the ball at the wall so that it hits it and rebounds, hopefully coming to a stop in the triangle. If one ball is already in the triangle, the next person can hit the wall and try to knock it out. The winner is the player with their ball left in at the end of the round. If there are four people, you play the best of four, and you all take turns at starting.

STONE RELEASE

This is a very simple game that is nevertheless extremely addictive. All you need are a few stones each that fit easily into your fist. In the soil or dirt track make a hole the size and shape of a cereal bowl. One person throws a stone into the hole from a distance of about 8 to 10 feet. The next person throws another to try to knock the first stone out. This simply goes on and on. If there is a stone in the hole you try to knock it out, if there isn't then you try to get one in the hole. Anything from two to six people is a nice number to play with. There is no need for everyone to stand in a line - you can move around the hole, but keeping your distance. Be careful of stones bouncing up at you. Round, smooth stones are best for this game.

MUD AND SAND PICTURES

This is one for artists and graffiti addicts. If you come across a sandpit or an area of mud, find a stick to make the area level so that you have a base to draw on or leave a message for someone; you could even make a 3D relief. You can use your hands or a stick to draw with. If the area is large enough, everyone can have a section to themselves. You can be really arty and roll in it or ride a bike over it - and don't forget the camera.

GROUND CAST

If you have ever watched a police detective film, you will probably have seen this process in action when there has been a break-in and the police want to get a cast of a footprint. This is done by mixing up some fine plaster and pouring it into the hole made in the mud. When it goes hard you lift the cast out, clean it up with water and cut away any plaster spillage. There are thousands of things you can take prints of, particularly animal tracks: dogs, foxes, birds, ducks, etc. If there is a city farm nearby, you could increase the types of animal footprints to include those of pigs, cows, horses and goats. You may be interested in car or bike tracks, drainhole covers, or anything else that will provide a good cast print. Why not make a display for your club or school?

ROAD SAFETY GAME

The idea of this game is to make young people more aware of road safety and the dangers of traffic. if you have a large area of tarmac and some lumps of chalk, mark out some streets with lots of junctions. This road layout should have traffic lights, crossings and other road markings. The young people on their push-bikes are shown how to approach junctions and use signals. You can go through many useful safety procedures. You may even set up an accident to show how things can go wrong. When the group is ready, transfer the skills to a real street. Make the game more fun by letting other children pretend to be traffic lights and road signs while waiting for a go on the bikes.

ART SPLAT

If your school art lessons have been getting a little dull, this should help you to express yourself more easily. Basically, you need to fill up lots of small plastic bags with liquid paint in different colours. Lay a large 6 by 10 foot piece of paper on the ground, or stick it firmly to an outside wall. Stand back and throw the bags at the paper so that they make wild and wonderful marks. If you want to extend the theme you could squirt paint with washing-up liquid bottles or water pistols. I recommend that you wear old clothes, use water-soluble paint and do it on waste land. You might even try to sell your artwork.

MOSAICS

Any object can be covered in mosaic, from a bottle to a brick wall. They are a lot of fun to do, from the designing stage, the finding of bits to use and the actual work, to the finished article. A mosaic can be very colourful, and of two or three dimensions. You can use traditional broken bits of tile or pottery or find a shop that sells the tiny square tiles. If you want to be really creative you can introduce domestic and other found objects to help build up a masterpiece. You could work on a picture, a pattern, or even make words, or it may be a school or club project to brighten up a wall. Mosaics will last for years if done properly. Find a book in the library on technique and method. Try to do it carefully over a few weeks rather than in a couple of hours.

CHESS AND DRAUGHTS

With chalk, mark out an area on the ground in the same layout as a chess board, but make it big enough for you to use tin cans, or even people, as playing pieces. For a draughts set you could have red Coke cans for one side and green Seven Up cans for the other. For a permanent set of pieces, fill the cans with plaster to give them weight.

WET SAND SCULPTURE

After a downpour of rain, sand becomes very clingy and sticks to itself, making it ideal material for sculpting. If there is no sand around, mud will do just as well. Each person has a plot of land and a set time to work on their sculpture. You can set a theme, or let them do anything they like. The sculptures can be made up purely of sand, or they can include the odd can or bit of wood. It's a good idea to take photos of them as soon as they are finished, and then leave them there for days and watch them crumble or wash away in the rain. If your city is by the sea and has a beach, you can watch the tide come in and crush them. If, for some stange reason, you have to destroy them as soon as you have finished, the winner has the privilege of jumping on all the other sculptures before anyone can jump on theirs. One theme you might use could be portraits of the club workers and you could film the destruction! Some playgrounds and building sites have lots of sand you could use with permission.